A BENN STUDY · DRAMA

THE NEW MERMAIDS

The Alchemist

THE NEW MERMAIDS

General Editor
BRIAN GIBBONS
Professor of English Literature, University of Leeds

The Alchemist

BEN JONSON

Edited by

DOUGLAS BROWN

Late Lecturer in English
University of Reading

LONDON/ERNEST BENN LIMITED

NEW YORK/W.W. NORTON AND COMPANY INC.

First published in this form 1966
by Ernest Benn Limited
12 Norwich Street, London, EC4A 1EƷ
& Sovereign Way, Tonbridge, Kent TN9 1RW
Second impression 1968
Third impression 1971
Fourth impression 1976
Fifth impression 1978
Sixth impression 1982
Seventh impression 1983

© *Ernest Benn Limited 1966*

Published in the United States of America by
W. W. Norton and Company Inc.
500 Fifth Avenue, New York, N.Y. 10110

Distributed in Canada by
The General Publishing Company Limited, Toronto

Printed in Great Britain

British Library Cataloguing in Publication Data

Jonson, Ben
  The alchemist. – (The new mermaids).
  I. Title   II. Brown, Douglas, b. 1921   III. Series
  882'3.   PR2605

ISBN 0–510–33606–X
ISBN 0–393–90014–2 (U.S.A.)

This edition was left unfinished by Douglas
Brown at his death in October 1964. The text
was completed, annotated, and introduced by
some of his colleagues at the University of
Reading, and seen through the press by
Brian Morris and Philip Brockbank

CONTENTS

ACKNOWLEDGEMENTS

The primary debt must, of course, be to the eleven volumes of *Ben Jonson*, edited by Herford and Simpson, which supplies almost everything any reader might need. Use has also been made of *The Alchemist*, edited C. M. Hathaway, Jr. (Yale Studies in English XVII) New York, 1903, *Eastward Hoe and The Alchemist*, edited F. E. Schelling (Belles Lettres Series), Boston, Mass., 1909, and *The Works*, edited Gifford, Cunningham, 9 vols., 1875.

INTRODUCTION

THE AUTHOR

BEN JONSON was born a Londoner in 1572, the posthumous son of an impoverished gentleman. His mother married a bricklayer shortly afterwards, and his circumstances in youth were decidedly straitened. Through the intervention of an outsider, however, he had some education at Westminster School under William Camden, who remained a lifelong friend; but he probably did not finish school and certainly did not go on, as most of his contemporaries there did, to Oxford or Cambridge. Instead he was apprenticed, probably in his stepfather's craft, about 1589, remaining in it long enough only to learn he 'could not endure' it. Before 1597 he had volunteered to serve in Flanders where, during a lull in the fighting, 'in the face of both the camps', he met and killed one of the enemy in single combat and returned from no-man's-land with his victim's weapons. The scene is an emblem for his life: the giant figure, a party to neither faction, warring alone in the classical manner before his awed onlookers.

Sometime in the early 1590s he married. By the time he was twenty-five he was playing the lead in Kyd's *Spanish Tragedy* for the theatrical manager and entrepreneur Philip Henslowe. As a writer he may also have composed additions to Kyd's work; he certainly did so for Nashe's satirical *Isle of Dogs*, and was imprisoned for the 'slandrous matter' in it. But already by 1598 Francis Meres listed him in *Palladis Tamia* amongst 'our best for tragedy' along with Kyd himself and Shakespeare. These tragedies, and indeed all the work of his early twenties, have vanished, but in the surviving records the man bursts upon the theatrical scene with characteristic and transforming energy.

In 1598 as well his first great success in comedy, *Every Man in his Humour*, was produced; in this, as in *Sejanus*, Shakespeare played a leading role. Within the same month Jonson killed an actor in Henslowe's company, Gabriel Spencer, in a duel. He pleaded guilty to a charge of felony and saved himself from the gallows only by claiming 'benefit of clergy', that is, by proving his literacy and hence immunity by reading 'neck-verse'. His goods—such as they may have been—were confiscated and he was branded on the thumb. His career was not yet fully under way: in writing of the incident, Henslowe refers to Jonson as a 'bricklayer'.

Still in the same year *The Case is Altered* was acted, once again

ix

with great success, and in 1599 or 1600 came *Every Man Out of his Humour*, which–although it too enhanced his growing reputation– included in the targets of its satire the diction of some contemporary playwrights, notably John Marston. Marston may have annoyed his older friend by a bungled attempt to flatter him in *Histriomastix* a few months earlier, but he was in any case ready to take very un- friendly revenge for *Every Man Out* when, in late 1600, he caricatured Jonson in *Jack Drum's Entertainment*. Jonson countered with *Cynthia's Revels*, Marston with *What You Will*, Jonson with *Poetaster*, all in 1601. Thomas Dekker, previously Jonson's collabora- tor on the lost tragedy *Page of Plymouth*, came to Marston's aid with *Satiro-mastix*. But Jonson had gone beyond attacking his attackers: his plays, and particularly *Poetaster*, satirized influential men, and he barely escaped prosecution again. He withdrew, not yet thirty years old, from comedy and the popular stage, into the patronage and protection first of Sir Robert Townshend and later Esmé Stewart, Lord Aubigny, to whom he dedicated the fruit of his retirement, *Sejanus*.

Once again Jonson's talent for trouble caused him difficulty with the authorities, this time on the pretext of 'popery and treason'– he had become a Catholic during his imprisonment for killing Spencer –and once again powerful friends intervened to save him. Still again in 1604, when he collaborated with his reconciled friend Marston and with George Chapman on the comedy *Eastward Ho!* he was jailed, now for satirizing the Scots, for James I was king. But once more he was let off, and on the whole the accession of James I was of great benefit to Jonson: for this brilliant and learned court he wrote almost all his many masques, delicate confections of erudition and artistry in which he knew no master.

But it is to *Volpone* (1605), *Epicoene* (1609–10), *The Alchemist* (1610), *Bartholomew Fair* (1614) and *The Devil is an Ass* (1616) that we must turn for the central documents of his comic maturity, interrupted only by the tragic (and unsuccessful) *Catiline* of 1611. Jonson had by 1612 become conscious of the scope of his accom- plishment, for in that year he began work on a collective edition which would enshrine in an impressive folio the authoritative text. His close connections with the court, doubtless enhanced when he gave up Catholicism about 1610, and the literary self-awareness begot by his huge reading in the classics, in part recorded in his common- place book *Timber*, led him, unique amongst the playwrights of his age, to take such pains with his *oeuvre*.

Jonson continued writing his masques and non-dramatic poems, but no stage play appeared after *The Devil is an Ass* until *The Staple of News* in 1625. Jonson's fortune declined in the nine years between. He began them with a walking tour to Scotland in 1618, where

Drummond recorded their *Conversations*, and with a visit to Oxford
in 1619, where the University made him a Master of Arts. He
ended them increasingly destitute of health, money and invention.
His rule over the 'tribe' that met at the Mermaid was unweakened,
but he depended more and more on pensions from Crown and City,
especially when he failed to maintain with Charles I the favour he
had found with the scholarly James I.

There followed *The New Inn* (1629), *The Magnetic Lady* (1632),
and *The Tale of a Tub* (1633); the first was a disaster the last two did
little to mitigate. Apart from a few verses he wrote nothing there-
after (his *English Grammar*, a draft of which perished in the fire that
destroyed his library in 1623, probably goes back to a period as
Professor of Rhetoric at Gresham College), although his lifelong
habit of reading was not broken. He did not complete work on the
second folio which was to include his writings since 1612. No child
of his survived him, and it fell to his intellectual disciples, the 'Sons
of Ben', to be his literary executors.

He died on 6th August, 1637, at the age of sixty-five, and was
buried in Westminster Abbey.

DATE AND SOURCES

The first performance of *The Alchemist* was by the King's Men at
the Globe in 1610. The exact date is not known, but the fact that
the play was entered on the Stationers' Register by Walter Burre on
3rd October, 1610,[1] indicates that the performance had taken place
by that date. Internal evidence like Ananias's confused chronology
at III.ii, 131–2, and V.v, 102–3 is unreliable, and the best evidence is
provided by the plague, which was in London from 12th July.[2] The
theatres must have been closed throughout the summer, and scholars
are now generally agreed that the first performance must have taken
place in the first half of the year.[3] Several passages in the play itself
suggest that the action was supposed to take place in the year 1610.
For example, Dame Pliant, who is said by Drugger to be 'But
nineteen, at the most', implies herself that she was born in 1591:

> Never, sin' eighty-eight could I abide 'em,
> And that was some three year afore I was born, in truth.
> (IV.iv, 29–30)

There is nothing to suggest a gap between composition and first
performance, and both may be assigned to the early months of 1610.

[1] Arber, *Transcript of the Stationers' Registers*, iii, 445.
[2] F. P. Wilson, *The Plague in Shakespeare's London*, 120–2.
[3] See E. K. Chambers, *The Elizabethan Stage*, iii, 371, and Herford and
Simpson, *Ben Jonson*, ix, 224.

Some confirmation of this date comes from the discovery that the King's Men took *The Alchemist* and *Othello* to Oxford in September on their autumn tour.[1]

The plot is entirely original. There is no 'source' in the sense of an existing story which Jonson adapted for his own purposes,[2] though impulses from many areas of his experience and learning come together within the play. There is no doubt, for example, that the idea of rogues carrying on their intrigues in the house of a man whose unexpected return provides the resolution of the plot comes from Plautus's *Mostellaria*; there are traces in the play of Erasmus's dialogue *De Alcumista*, which Jonson probably read at school; Delrio's *Disquisitiones Magicae* provides much of the alchemical argument, and Broughton's *A Concent of Scripture* is ransacked to produce Dol's distraction in IV.v. Similarly, it has been argued that Surly is a development of the character of Bonario in *Volpone*, that Subtle is in some ways very like Volpone himself, and that Face is deeply indebted to Mosca. There is some truth in all this, just as Jonson could not have been unaware of contemporary alchemists and tricksters like John Dee, Edward Kelly and Simon Forman when creating Subtle and Face.[3] But this is only to say that no work of art can be created *ex nihilo*. Jonson's erudite mind and observant eye have synthesized the materials of his experience into a totality which is greater than the sum of them all.

THE PLAY

The time is come about, whereof *Diogenes* prophesied; when he gave the reason why he would be buried grovelling: we have made the earth's bottom powerful to the lofty skies: Gold that lay buried in the buttock of the world: is now made the head and ruler of the people:

(Feltham, *Resolves*)

Seek not Proud *Riches*, but such as thou mayest get justly, use soberly, distribute cheerfully, and leave contentedly . . . The *ways to enrich* are many, and most of them Foul.

(Bacon, *Of Riches*)

[1] The discovery was made in the Fulman papers of Corpus Christi College, Oxford, by Geoffrey Tillotson. See *The Times Literary Supplement*, 20th July, 1933.
[2] Ariosto's *Negromante* (1520) and Lyly's *Gallathea* may confidently be dismissed, but a case for Bruno's *Candelaio* (an Italian play published in Paris in 1582) has been made by Professor C. G. Child, in the New York *Nation*, 28th July, 1904. The claim is discussed and dismissed by Herford and Simpson (*Ben Jonson*, ii, 94–98) who give a summary of the plot as Appendix VI to the same volume.
[3] These points are discussed at length in the edition of *The Alchemist* by C. M. Hathaway (New York, 1903), 90–103; Herford and Simpson, though agreeing for the most part, find some of his conclusions unacceptable.

The Alchemist is a play about Avarice, and the symbol of Avarice is gold. It is this *cupiditas* which unites the cozeners and the cozened, which places Subtle and Lovewit on the same side of the moral fence, which motivates in various degrees and directions the whole complex of actions out of which the play is built. Jonson, as critic of the acquisitive society, is concerned to explore the rich variety of ways in which human energies and ingenuity can be directed towards the processes of enrichment. In his critique of Avarice he is rehearsing one of the great commonplaces of literature in the special terms of his own age; Chaucer had shown long ago, in *The Pardoner's Tale*, that 'radix malorum est cupiditas', and Molière would later point the same moral in *L'Avare*. But Renaissance writers had many ways of presenting Avarice, ranging in mode from the drama to the emblem, from the sermon to the hieroglyph, and Jonson's play represents one kind of moral picture among many.

The faces of greed

In the masques and entertainments of the seventeenth century allegories of virtue and vice are usually presented by actors, who, by their dress and appearance, inform the audience of what they represent. Certain conventions of presentation had been inherited from the Middle Ages, and even from antiquity, and these had been assembled and codified by Renaissance encyclopaedists, of whom perhaps the most important is Cesare Ripa. The first edition of Ripa's *Iconologia* was published in Rome in 1593, and by 1603 it had reached a third edition in which a number of descriptions of virtues and vices were added, together with some illustrations. The edition of 1613 was further augmented by the author, and others followed in 1618, 1620, 1625, 1630 and later years. Poets and painters, although much of the material was already familiar to them, found the *Iconologia* a useful handbook, and Jonson is known to have used a copy of the 1603 edition in his own masques. One of the five descriptions of Avarice which Ripa gives runs: 'A woman badly dressed, bare-headed, bare-footed, holding a toad in her right hand and a closed purse in her left',[1] and in Jonson's masque *The Golden Age Restored* (1615) the Iron Age enters and calls up Avarice as the 'grandame Vice of all my issue'. Jonson used Ripa's pictures and descriptions in many ways, sometimes following closely, sometimes inventing, sometimes combining the attributes of two figures in his description of a third, but always using visual images to present moral qualities, and this visual presentation of Avarice is part of the tradition.

The word Jonson most commonly uses for the symbolical figure

[1] Illustrations from Ripa may be found among the plates in Gilbert's *The Symbolic Persons in the Masques of Ben Jonson*, North Carolina, 1948.

or object is *hieroglyphic*, which he explains himself in *The Masque of Beauty* when he describes the rose as the 'hieroglyphic of splendour', and pearls and lilies as 'the special hieroglyphics of loveliness'. One of the most important books to which Jonson had recourse in this phase of his career was Pierio Valeriano's *Hieroglyphica*, first published in Latin in 1556 and translated into Italian in 1602. Valeriano lists a large number of hieroglyphics, from the lion, the serpent, the elephant, to the moon, the head, and the anchor, and shows how each one represents a wide variety of human qualities and activities. In Book XXXV, 'De Manu', he describes the hand as the hieroglyphic of Avarice:

> . . . There are also people who paint the left hand alone, with clenched fingers, as the mark of graspingness and avarice; interpreters also give the left hand as the mark of money and increase in property, for the left hand is more appropriate for guarding things, since it is less active (than the right) and better fitted to graspingness.[1]

Valeriano's hieroglyphics are derived from classical sources and not, as the name suggests, from Egyptian, but the method of presentation is constant: the hieroglyph is the mute symbol of the quality. As A. H. Gilbert has said: 'In *The Masque of Blackness* the hieroglyphics, such as the salamander and the urn sphered with wine, indicate the "qualities" of their bearers, such as majesty and purity'.[2] Valeriano was not the only encyclopaedist interested in this form of symbolism, but he was among the best known, and since Jonson is known to have used him he may stand as a representative.

Even more numerous were the emblem writers.[3] All over Europe emblem books were published and reprinted for a seemingly insatiable public. An emblem was a drawing or picture expressing an abstract quality, or a class of persons, or a fable, or an allegory, and usually accompanied by explanatory verses. In England the best known emblem writers were probably Geoffrey Whitney, whose *Choice of Emblemes* was published at Leyden in 1586, and (later) Francis Quarles, whose *Emblems* appeared in 1635 and were constantly reprinted. On the continent, one of the most influential collections was that made by Andrea Alciati, which first appeared in the middle of the sixteenth century, and was many times reprinted. Alciati has several emblems depicting Avarice, and the first of them, Emblem LXXXIV, shows a landscape with a stream flowing through it, and Tantalus up to his armpits in the water

---

[1] Neque desunt qui manum tantum sinistram digitis compressis pro tenacitate et auaritia pingant: nam et coniectores laeuam lucri, et augendae rei signum ponunt, quippe que ad custodiendum magis idonea sit vtpote segnior, et tenacitati accomodatior.
[2] *Symbolic Persons*, 6.
[3] See R. Freeman, *English Emblem Books*, 1948.

reaching for fruit from a branch which hangs down over his head. Beneath the picture are four lines of Latin which comment on the situation:

The wretched Tantalus stands thirstily in the midst of the waters, and although he is hungry he cannot reach the fruit which is so close to him. Change the name, miser, and the story will be true of you; you no more enjoy your possessions than if you did not possess them at all.[1]

Alciati goes on to analyse and apply picture and comment for several pages, drawing examples from Petronius, Horace, Achilles Statius and others. Don Cameron Allen has shown[2] that Jonson made use of Alciati on at least one occasion (*Poetaster*, V.iii, 101–3), and the emblematic presentation of Avarice could be illustrated from a dozen different writers. The habit of thinking about abstract qualities in visual images was widespread and deep-rooted, and the multiplicity of iconologies, hieroglyphics, and emblems bear witness to the strength and range of the tradition.

It is against this background that the pageant of Avarice in Jonson's play should be seen. He is concerned to display the various facets of greed in his chosen social context, a context which is sharply limited and constrained. It has often been pointed out how close Jonson comes in *The Alchemist* to a strict observation of the so-called 'unities' of time, place, and action, but the dramaturgical austerity goes deeper than a mere control of surface plot. The characters, and especially the dupes, are each a brilliant compromise between realism and abstraction; outside the confines of Lovewit's house Surly and Mammon would have nothing to say to one another, but here they and the others set up a momentary pattern of desires and energies which shatters when they touch. Kastril and Drugger display Avarice at its most venial, at its lowest pitch of intensity. Kastril wants no more than an entry into 'good company' by learning how to take the altitude of a quarrel (III.iv), while Drugger is doing no more than cutting the corners in his pursuit of a lawful, if lowly, trade. Dapper stands on a higher rung in the ladder of Avarice, but his search for gold is still oblique; he is the gamester, the 'sporting man' whose greed is cheerful. He desires a fly 'for all games' but only for games, and his ambition rises no higher than 'But I do think, now, I shall leave the law'. He is superbly 'placed' in Face's description of him:

[1]   Heu miser in mediis sitiens stat Tantalus undis,
        Et poma esuriens proxima habere nequit.
     Nomine mutato de te id dicetur auare,
        Qui, quasi non habeas, non frueris quod habes.
[2] 'Ben Jonson and the Hieroglyphics', *Philological Quarterly*, XVIII (1939), 290–300.

> . . . a special gentle,
> That is the heir to forty marks, a year,
> Consorts with the small poets of the time,
> Is the sole hope of his old grandmother,
> That knows the law, and writes you six fair hands . . .

Such a man's Avarice is modest, pitiful, and his reward is apt—a gingerbread gag. Quarles once described an emblem as 'a silent parable', and the three figures of Kastril, Drugger and Dapper, though sharply and widely distinguished, are emblems and parables of Avarice, rather than Avarice personified.

Ananias and Tribulation are altogether larger figures—we have moved from the world of Alciati to the world of Valeriano and Ripa. Jonson, who professed himself a Catholic during the decade before he wrote this play, treats them with notable contempt—the more so because their Avarice is solemn, pretentious, hypocritical. They are arrogant, and Jonson understood arrogance. He exposes and deflates Puritan greed by a delicate and totally dramatic satiric device: he brings the Puritan and the Alchemist together, and shows they are one and the same:

SUBTLE   . . . Who are you?
ANANIAS
  A faithful Brother, if it please you.
SUBTLE   What's that?
  A Lullianist? A Ripley? *Filius artis*?
  Can you sublime, and dulcify? Calcine?
  Know you the *sapor pontic*? *Sapor styptic*?
  Or, what is homogene, or heterogene?
ANANIAS
  I understand no heathen language, truly.

                                        (II.v, 6–12)

The key-word is 'Brother', which Ananias offers in a religious sense, and Subtle accepts as meaning a member of the alchemical fraternity. Suddenly the two frauds are identified, and in the later debates between Subtle, Ananias and Tribulation Jonson relentlessly presses home the identity, crowning it with the ironical recital (III.ii) of Puritan practices, from which possession of the stone will liberate them. In these two figures Jonson exposes the face of greed at its most ugly. Jonson's art must be judged in terms of pattern and colour, and the Puritans are set forward as the moral nadir of the play, Avarice in its blackest suit.

Mammon, on the other hand, is the play's most colourful figure; the gargantuan quality of his greed is matched by the damasked extravagance of his invention. He is non-realistic, unbelievable, and he is only viable as a dramatic character because he is underwritten and guaranteed by the credible ambitiousness of Kastril, Drugger and Dapper. Herford and Simpson point up the Marlowesque quality of his hyperbole when they describe him as 'a Faustus of the senses', and this insight is shrewdly developed by Levin, who says:

Marlowe consistently presented the voluptuary as a hero; to Jonson, he is always either a villain like Volpone, or a dupe like Sir Epicure Mammon . . . Jonson could not have expressed his reservations more explicitly, nor hit upon a more elaborate contrivance for turning to dust and ashes all the lovely fruit of the Renaissance imagination.[1]

As an image of Avarice Mammon is a marvellously ambivalent figure. Jonson manipulates his audience's responses adroitly, so that moral disapproval is unbalanced by admiration for the wit, the imaginative energy, and, above all, the teeming fecundity of invention. Mammon's greed is a dream, and the dream liberates both the imagination and the moral sense. It is in this that Jonson, as a dramatist, can enter a dimension denied to the iconologists and the emblem writers, whose figures, once created, are unalterable and patient only of ethical application. Mammon enters the play as a stage figure–he is a man as we are–and he grows into a superman dreaming up his Elysium before our eyes.

Subtle, Face and Dol contribute little to the play's exposure of Avarice; they are the clear-sighted exploiters of the Avarice of others, sublimely careless of the perils attendant on their own greed. From the point of view of orthodox morality they are rogues and tricksters, but Jonson invites our admiration for the very vigour of their trickery, and their infinite resourcefulness in action. Primarily, they escape our calumny because they are self-confessed cheats, and the targets of Jonson's satire in *The Alchemist* are the pretentious and the hypocrites. Subtle, Face and Dol have few illusions about themselves or about each other, and their Avarice is open, not to say blatant. It is as if Jonson's spleen is raised not so much by the grasping fingers of Tantalus, as by the clenched fingers in Valeriano's description.

Surly should be the ethical arbitrator of the play. He, like Asper in *Every Man Out of his Humour*, is the exposer of vice and folly; he represents the golden mean between sharp practice and green innocence; he is the man who 'would not be gulled'. Yet Jonson allows him no status. He is no match for Subtle in argument, and at the very moment when he seems to have all the schemers in his hand, and to be about to reap his modest reward, he is foiled by Lovewit and despatched into discomfiture with the other dupes and rascals. There are dramatic reasons for this, but for the moment it is enough to observe that the absence of vicious qualities, in particular of

[1] Harry Levin, 'An Introduction to Ben Jonson', reprinted in *Ben Jonson: A Collection of Critical Essays*, ed. Barish, New Jersey, 1963, 52.

Avarice, is not enough to establish any kind of heroic stature in this play. More, we see that virtue, in itself, is powerless.

In the morality of the play there are no positives. It is Thersites' world–'such patchery, such juggling, and such knavery'[1]–yet the total impression is of a vast expenditure of energy (it is an exhausting play to watch) and nothing to show for it. The figures of greed which Jonson creates may be icons of Avarice in one sense, but they are never static; they are forever grasping, getting, spending, losing. The moral discovery which *The Alchemist* makes is concerned with the sheer *waste* which Avarice implies. The world is constantly present; getting and spending we lay waste our powers.

Comic Justice

The fifth act provides a series of verdicts upon the action. In *Volpone* Jonson had imposed a rigorous justice upon the evildoers in a court scene which sternly eschewed both charity and wit. The effect of this judgement is to enforce with great power the sense of evil and suffering which the preceding comic tones had largely masked. The end of *Volpone* declares unequivocally that the game is over, the chickens have come home to roost, and whatsoever a man sows that shall he reap. Such Levitical justice was no part of Jonson's purpose in *The Alchemist*. The comedy of *The Alchemist* is delicate, and it requires delicate resolution. In *Volpone* the fibres are of a darker and stronger twist, which can sustain the more nearly tragic vision at the end.

Yet the judgements in *The Alchemist* form a wry kind of justice. Its world is not without dangers. We should not forget the plague which hangs over the house, nor that laboratory explosions are apt to injure people, nor the angry mob pounding at the door. The cart and the whip are present fears to Dol, and quite early in the play the perils which awaited the conjurer and the false coiner are firmly established. These presences are latent rather than manifest in the action, but they serve to keep the fantasy in touch with the social realities, they constitute a yardstick by which intentions and activities might be judged. The rejection of this yardstick is one of the notable abstentions of the play. Jonson's judge is not an official representative of order and authority, but Lovewit, the 'jovy boy', 'not hide-bound', who loves a teeming wit as he loves his nourishment. This arbitrator is akin to the Justice who dispenses the rewards and punishments at the end of *Every Man in his Humour*, but whereas that play is concerned with comparatively harmless misunderstandings and fooleries *The Alchemist* has to do with crimes.

Lovewit enters with an air of authority–'Has there been such

[1] *Troilus and Cressida*, II. iii.

resort, say you?'—which immediately breaks down into curiosity as
he smells a device:

> What should my knave advance,
> To draw this company? He hung out no banners
> Of a strange calf, with five legs, to be seen?
> Or a huge lobster, with six claws?

(V.i, 6–9)

His subsequent actions form a kind of 'moral slide' as he descends
from investigator to bargainer to trickster to exploiter. The
stations of the slide are clearly marked in his conversations with the
neighbours, with the dupes, with Face over the terms of the bargain,
and with Surly over the fate of Dame Pliant. The fifth act, which
should see the revoking of the comic licence and the re-establishment
of order, becomes a comic exploit in its own right, with Lovewit as
protagonist and manipulator. Here again Jonson's economy is match-
less. Lovewit's settlement with Face begets all the other judgements
almost mechanically: Surly is foiled, the other dupes are all sent
penniless away, Subtle and Dol disappear over the garden wall, with
Face speeding the parting jest:

> Let's know where you set up next; I'll send you
> A customer, now and then, for old acquaintance:

Face himself is the only survivor, and he divides the spoils (un-
equally it is true) with Lovewit. Face, the play's prime manipulator
and greatest rogue, is vindicated by his wit; the wicked and slothful
servant enters into the joy of his lord. Thus the verdict in which the
play comes to rest is an exaltation of Intelligence above virtue, in
which the honest Surly is abashed while the impudent Face triumphs.
Edmund Wilson has described it well:

There is no element of false morality to blur Jonson's acrid relish of
the confidence games of his rogues: the cynicism is carried right
through.[1]

'Cynicism' is a strong word, and Wilson was arguing a special case,
but we have only to compare Lovewit's pardon of Face with the
Duke's judgement of Lucio in *Measure for Measure* to appreciate
the difference between Shakespeare's conception of comic justice
and Jonson's. In *The Alchemist* Intelligence is at a premium, and
creative ingenuity assumes the stature of a virtue: unto him that
hath shall be given, and he shall have abundance. If we take this as
a summing up of the human condition it seems both harsh and super-
ficial. But if we see it as the savage judgement upon a viciously acquisitive society, a society where Avarice is regnant and rampant,

[1] Edmund Wilson, 'Morose Ben Jonson' in *The Triple Thinkers*, and reprinted in *Ben Jonson: A Collection of Critical Essays*, ed. Barish, 63.

where Alchemist and Puritan serve the same gods, it becomes
acceptable. Instead of bringing the play's fantasy to rest on a solid
ground of moral certainties Jonson has judged it by its own rules,
and on its own terms. His verdict is that the acquisitive society is a
vortex of greed, competition, self-seeking, out-manoeuvring, corner-
cutting, swindling and cozening; its justice is unpredictable and
arbitrary, and cleverness is its only virtue. But it is as it is. You
must take it or leave it.

The Clash of Jargons

It was Coleridge who spoke of Jonson's 'sterling English diction',[1]
and in a play like *The Alchemist* which offers a staggering display of
the uses of language this is a point to bear in mind. Indeed, the
range of language might be plotted between the 'sterling English'
and the total gibberish of Dol's fit of talking in IV.v. The tone
which Coleridge admired is set early in the first act:

> But I shall put you in mind, sir, at Pie Corner,
> Taking your meal of steam in, from cooks' stalls,
> Where, like the Father of Hunger, you did walk
> Piteously costive, with your pinched-horn-nose,
> And your complexion, of the Roman wash,
> Stuck full of black, and melancholic worms,
> Like powder corns, shot, at th'artillery-yard.

                                              (I.i, 25–31)

'Pie Corner' and 'th'artillery-yard' root the statements in actual,
London places; they give a local habitation to the speech. This is the
same impulse as Horace displays in those Odes which celebrate the
Roman countryside, the famous *fons Bandusiae*, or, by contrast,
the seventh Ode of Book I:

> Laudabunt alii claram Rhodon aut Mytilenen
>   aut Epheson bimarisve Corinthi
> moenia vel Baccho Thebas vel Apolline Delphos
>   insignes aut Thessala Tempe.

Levin quotes examples to show how Jonson elsewhere paraphrased
the tropes of Catullus into Rumney and the Chelsea fields.[2] It is
this locative impulse, attended by a sensitive simplicity of diction
and allusion which allows the light colloquialisms their proper
assertion, that goes to make up the basic speech of Jonsonian
comedy and serves as a touchstone for the more complex uses of
language elsewhere in the play.

The powerful extravagance of Dol's raving has already been
mentioned, but the more subtle, and totally dramatic mode of
speech can perhaps best be illustrated from Mammon's first speech

[1] *Lectures on Shakespeare* (Bohn edition), 397.
[2] In *Ben Jonson &c.*, ed. Barish, 44.

in II.i. L. C. Knights has shown[1] how what begins as comic in-
flation and fantastic caricature develops through a series of negatives into a richly ambiguous statement about the social world and
the world of alchemy. Perhaps it is even more than that. Mammon,
when he enters his dream, when he sets his foot on shore 'In *novo
orbe*' takes Surly with him, and it is to convince Surly, the sceptic,
that the string of negatives roll forth, culminating in the powerful,
persuasive allusion which unites the Inn yard with the book of
Exodus:

> No more
> Shall thirst of satin, or the covetous hunger
> Of velvet entrails, for a rude-spun cloak,
> To be displayed at Madam Augusta's, make
> The sons of sword, and hazard fall before
> The golden calf, and on their knees, whole nights,
> Commit idolatry with wine, and trumpets:

This is the strong-knit, allusive tone, which is frequently sounded in
the play, and which is the particular voice of Mammon. It modulates
further in the same scene, when to the jibes of Surly are added the
blandishments of Face. Both speakers are brief, and the effect of
their presences and words is principally to incite Mammon to screw
up his rhetoric and invention to ever higher notes, so that the language of comedy in this scene separates out on to three levels, the
crude realism of Surly ('The decayed Vestals of Pict-Hatch would
thank you'), Face's smooth civility ('The evening will set red, upon
you, sir'), and over all the swelling chant of Mammon's personal
gloria.

These uses of language, the plain and the ornate, are found for
the most part in the first two acts. The language of the middle of the
play is more violent. In the third and fourth acts it becomes drama-
tically important that people shall not properly understand what is
said to them, and that they shall be mystified, frightened, or im-
pressed with their failure to comprehend. Jonson's art accomplishes
this by clashing together the various jargons which have already
been established: the vast sprawl of technical terms which surround
alchemy had been used to suppress the loquacity of Mammon in
II.iii, and in II.v it is employed again, liturgically, in a catechistical
exchange between Subtle and Face to baffle and control the thrus-
tingness of Ananias:

SUBTLE
> Sirrah, my varlet, stand you forth, and speak to him
> Like a philosopher: answer, i' the language.

[1] 'Ben Jonson, Dramatist', in *Penguin Guide to English Literature*, ed. Boris
Ford, ii, 312–4.

Name the vexations, and the martyrizations
Of metals, in the work.
FACE   Sir, Putrefaction,
Solution, Ablution, Sublimation,
Cohobation, Calcination, Ceration, and
Fixation.

It is the episcopal pomp of this jargon which puts down the humble 'saint'.

The opposition is renewed in the opening scenes of Act Three. Here Jonson allows the two Puritans a scene to themselves in which to develop the separatist tropes, and they create a language of Amsterdam which is grave and impressive, rich in its biblical sonorities:–'In pure zeal', 'the language of Canaan', 'profane person', 'The visible mark of the Beast', 'holy cause', 'sanctified cause', 'sanctified course', 'The children of perdition'. The first hundred lines of the following scene (III.ii) present the attempt of Tribulation to make some kind of verbal contact with Subtle. Each of them chastens his speech, tempers his jargon, in order to communicate. But Ananias cannot be contained, and bursts out with the party line and the party slogans: 'I hate traditions: I do not trust 'em', 'They are popish, all'. Subtle and Tribulation draw back, and Subtle sets up again the impregnable rock of his jargon:

We must now increase
Our fire to *ignis ardens*, we are past
Fimus equinus, balnei, cineris,
And all those lenter heats.

Tribulation resorts to casuistic chop-logic about the relative legality of coining and casting, and as the scene ends he finds refuge in an appeal to authority, like a trade-union official going off to consult his executive:

I'll make a question of it, to the Brethren.

Jonson uses the clash of jargons to prevent communication. The high-sounding terms are impressive, but they are simply counters in a struggle for ascendancy. In scenes like this between the Alchemist and the Puritans the words, far from linking people together, drive them apart. The play has other scenes in which this movement takes place–Mammon's wooing of Dol, Subtle and Kastril on the causes of quarrels, and (in its most complex form) Subtle and Face in conversation with the disguised Surly, whose Spanish, though incomprehensible to them, is infinitely suggestive. The effect of the play's various powerful jargons is to prevent, or baffle, or mutilate meaningful communication between characters whenever the dramaturgy requires that communication should be stifled. There is a constantly recurring sense in the play of the unbridgeable distance between people; they stand, shouting at each other across the abyss.

The Metaphor of Change

The central image of the play is the figure of transmutation; the end of all things is the search for gold. Yet the image is flexible and expansive because the end of the search is an *ignis fatuus*, an illusion. In *Volpone*, the gold is real enough, a present and potent force in the action, but in *The Alchemist* all the characters are chasing a will o' the wisp. It is perhaps this very lack of substance in the search which allows the dramatist such freedom in his exploration of the image. To return for a moment to Mammon's speech in II.i, the key is provided by the line which Subtle speaks to introduce him:

If his dream last, he'll turn the age, to gold.

This was the quest of the genuine alchemist, and despite the chicanery and pretentiousness which surrounded the pseudo-science the motives of many of its practitioners were altruistic and laudable. The alchemist had a place and a real status in Elizabethan society because an age of such scientific curiosity and economic aggressiveness could not afford to neglect the possibility of turning base metals to gold.[1] Mammon's speech, for all its delusions of grandeur and adoration of excess, displays a wide generosity; everyone will benefit when he has the philosopher's stone. The 'hollow dye' and the 'frail card' will no longer be needed, and men will be able to live without deception. This expansive movement towards a vision of the Golden Age is part of the metaphor of change within the speech, but counterpointing it, balancing it, is the ethical descent from the noble to the base. As the metal is purified and refined by fire into gold, so humanity is consumed by the growing fire of lust and concupiscence, and the vision of the Golden Age degenerates into dull Aretine's pictures. But the image of metamorphosis is not confined to the language of the play. In visual terms it is a constant procession of shifts and disguises: Face becomes the Captain who becomes Jeremy, Dol takes on the mantle of the Queen of Faery, Surly is disguised as the Diego, everyone is striving to become someone else. The final impression of the play is of an immense activity, a constant flux of language and spectacle, of things changing and being changed. There is chemical alchemy and there is human alchemy, yet it is Jonson's triumph that despite all the disguises and transformations, identities are preserved. In its dominant preoccupation with Avarice through the processes of alchemy *The*

[1] The best account of alchemists and alchemy in this play is given in the Introduction to Hathaway's edition of *The Alchemist*, New York, 1903.

Alchemist emerges as a vast gloss upon the reply of Marlowe's Bashaw in *The Jew of Malta,* when the Governor asks him 'What wind drives you thus into Malta rhode?'

The wind that bloweth all the world besides,
Desire of gold.

NOTE ON THE TEXT

The play was printed in a quarto (Q) in 1612 and in the collective folio (F) edition in 1616, both under Jonson's supervision and incorporating press corrections. Jonson's hand is not so clear in the posthumous second folio (F2) of 1640 on which he had done some work before he died.

This edition follows the corrected state of F. Some passages which might have given offence were altered in F; these and other substantial differences are mentioned in notes save when, as often, Q omits a stage direction. The spelling, including capitalization and the contrast of roman with italic, small capital and black letter types, is modernized throughout, as is the presentation of speeches. In F block entries precede every scene, and the first name among them is that of the first speaker. In this edition entries are supplied only as the action requires, and the first speaker has a separate speech prefix. Speech prefixes in broken lines are all on the left; Jonson had them within the line:

Dare you do this? SUB. Yes faith, yes faith. FAC. Why! Who (I.i, 12).

Abbreviations are expanded, and so are elisions within (but not between) words, but forms reflecting the colloquial speech of the time have been retained.

The punctuation follows Jonson's highly-developed system for F, considerably more explicit than Q, except that a few obvious errors have been silently corrected; the metrical apostrophe, intended to prevent elision of vowels in adjacent words, has been omitted; and the use of hyphens has been modernized.

FURTHER READING

The Jonson bibliography is vast, and the following brief list is intended only to facilitate the pursuit of some of the issues raised in the Introduction and Notes.

Barish, J. A., *Ben Jonson and the Language of Prose Comedy*, Cambridge, Mass., 1960.

Barish, J. A., ed., *Ben Jonson: A Collection of Critical Essays* (Twentieth Century Views), New Jersey, 1963.

Blissett, William, Julian Patrick, and R. W. Van Fossen, edd., *A Celebration of Ben Jonson*, Toronto and London, 1973.

Davies, Robertson, 'Ben Jonson and Alchemy', *Stratford Papers 1968–69*, ed. B. A. W. Jackson, Shannon, 1972, pp. 40–60.

Dessen, Alan C., *Jonson's Moral Comedy*, Evanston, Ill., 1971.

Donaldson, Ian, *The World Upside-Down*, Oxford, 1970.

Eliot, T. S., 'Ben Jonson', reprinted in *Elizabethan Dramatists*, 1963.

Ellis-Fermor, U., *The Jacobean Drama*, fourth edition with additional material, 1961.

Gilbert, A. H., *The Symbolic Persons in the Masques of Ben Jonson*, Duke University Press, North Carolina, 1948.

Hibbard, G. R., ed., *The Elizabethan Theatre, IV*, Toronto, London and Basingstoke, 1974.

Kernan, Alvin B., ed., *The Alchemist*, New Haven and London, 1974.

Kernan, Alvin B., 'Alchemy and Acting: the Major Plays of Ben Jonson', in *Ben Jonson: Quadricentennial Essays*, ed. Mary Olive Thomas, Atlanta, 1973.

Knights, L. C., *Drama and Society in the Age of Jonson*, 1937.

Partridge, E. B., *The Broken Compass, A Study of the Major Comedies of Ben Jonson*, New York, 1958.

Sackton, A. H., *Rhetoric as a Dramatic Language in Ben Jonson*, New York, 1948.

Thayer, C. G., *Ben Jonson: Studies in the Plays*, Norman, Okla., 1963.

THE
ALCHEMIST.

A Comœdie.

Acted in the yeere 1610. By the
Kings MAIESTIES
Seruants.

The Author B. I.

LVCRET.

————*petere inde coronam,*
Vnde prius nulli velarint tempora Musa.

LONDON,

Printed by WILLIAM STANSBY

M. DC. XVI.

TO THE LADY, MOST
DESERVING HER NAME,
AND BLOOD:
Mary,
LADY WROTH

MADAM,

In the age of sacrifices, the truth of religion was not in the greatness, and fat of the offerings, but in the devotion, and zeal of the sacrificers: else, what could a handful of gums have done in the sight of a hecatomb? Or, how might I appear at this altar, except with those affections, that no less love the light and witness, than they have the conscience of your virtue? If what I offer bear an acceptable odour, and hold the first strength, it is your value of it, which remembers, where, when, and to whom it was kindled. Otherwise, as the times are, there comes rarely forth that thing, so full of authority, or example, but by assiduity and custom, grows less, and loses. This, yet, safe in your judgment (which is a Sidney's) is forbidden to speak more; lest it talk, or look like one of the ambitious faces of the time: who, the more they paint, are the less themselves.

> Your Ladyship's true honourer,
> Ben Jonson.

Mary, Lady Wroth. The name is also spelled 'Worth' – hence 'most deserving her name'. She was the eldest daughter of the first Earl of Leicester, niece of Sir Philip Sidney, and married Sir Robert Wroth at Penshurst on 27th September, 1604.
1–5 See Seneca, *De Beneficiis*, I.vi.2

If thou beest more, thou art an understander, and then I trust thee. If thou art one that takest up, and but a pretender, beware at what hands thou receivest thy commodity; for thou wert never more fair in the way to be cozened (than in this age) in poetry, especially in plays: wherein, now, the concupiscence of dances, and antics so reigneth, as to run away from nature, and be afraid of her, is the only point of art that tickles the spectators. But how out of purpose, and place, do I name art? When the professors are grown so obstinate contemners of it, and presumers on their own naturals, as they are deriders of all diligence that way, and, by simple mocking at the terms, when they understand not the things, think to get off wittily with their ignorance. Nay, they are esteemed the more learned, and sufficient for this, by the many, through their excellent vice of judgment. For they commend writers, as they do fencers, or wrestlers; who if they come in robustiously, and put for it with a great deal of violence, are received for the braver fellows: when many times their own rudeness is the cause of their disgrace, and a little touch of their adversary gives all that boisterous force the foil. I deny not, but that these men, who always seek to do more than enough, may some time happen on something that is good, and great; but very seldom: and when it comes it doth not recompense the rest of their ill. It sticks out perhaps, and is more eminent, because all is sordid, and vile about it: as lights are more discerned in a thick darkness, than a faint shadow. I speak not this, out of a hope to do good on any man, against his will; for I know, if it were put to the question of theirs, and mine, the worse would find more suffrages: because the most favour common errors. But I give thee this warning, that there is a great difference between those, that (to gain the opinion of copie) utter all they can, however unfitly; and those that use election, and a mean. For it is only the disease of the unskilful, to think rude things greater than polished: or scattered more numerous than composed.

To the Reader
>   These critical comments on the popular contempt for art are paralleled in Jonson's *Discoveries* (see Herford and Simpson, *Ben Jonson*, viii, 572) and derive ultimately from Quintilian.

THE PERSONS OF THE PLAY

SUBTLE, The Alchemist
FACE, The Housekeeper
DOL COMMON,
   Their Colleague
DAPPER, A Clerk
DRUGGER, A Tobaccoman
LOVEWIT, Master of the House

EPICURE MAMMON,
   A Knight
SURLY, A Gamester
TRIBULATION, A Pastor
   of Amsterdam
ANANIAS, A Deacon there
KASTRIL, The Angry Boy
DAME PLIANT,
   His Sister: A Widow

Neighbours
Officers
Mutes

The Scene

LONDON [, inside Lovewit's house and in the street outside]

Surly. He is addressed as 'Pertinax' (i.e. obstinate) at II.i,79, and II.ii, 5. He, like Quarlous in *Bartholomew Fair*, is described as a 'Gamester', which usually implied dissolute life as well as gambling.

Ananias. According to Sir Charles Firth the name Ananias, from this play, became the accepted nickname for a Puritan. The Puritans' use of biblical names for their children was justified on the grounds that since all are tainted with original sin, children might be named after any sinner mentioned in the Bible. The Ananias 'that cozened the Apostles' is found in *Acts*, v, but there is another, and better, Ananias in *Acts*, ix, 10 ff.

Mutes. As Herford and Simpson point out (*Ben Jonson*, x, 54) Officers and Neighbours are specified, so that only the Chaplain of V.iv,99 remains. Perhaps he walks out with Lovewit at the opening of V.v.

The Alchemist

THE ARGUMENT

T he sickness hot, a master quit, for fear,
H is house in town: and left one servant there.
E ase him corrupted, and gave means to know
A cheater, and his punk; who, now brought low,
L eaving their narrow practice, were become 5
C ozeners at large: and, only wanting some
H ouse to set up, with him they here contract,
E ach for a share, and all begin to act.
M uch company they draw, and much abuse,
I n casting figures, telling fortunes, news, 10
S elling of flies, flat bawdry, with the stone:
T ill it, and they, and all in fume are gone.

PROLOGUE

Fortune, that favours fools, these two short hours
   We wish away; both for your sakes, and ours,
Judging spectators: and desire in place,
   To th'author justice, to ourselves but grace.
Our scene is London, 'cause we would make known,   5
   No country's mirth is better than our own.
No clime breeds better matter, for your whore,
   Bawd, squire, imposter, many persons more,
Whose manners, now called humours, feed the stage:
   And which have still been subject, for the rage   10
Or spleen of comic writers. Though this pen
   Did never aim to grieve, but better men;
Howe'er the age, he lives in, doth endure
   The vices that she breeds, above their cure.
But, when the wholesome remedies are sweet,   15
   And, in their working, gain, and profit meet,
He hopes to find no spirit so much diseased,
   But will, with such fair correctives be pleased.
For here, he doth not fear, who can apply.
   If there be any, that will sit so nigh   20
Unto the stream, to look what it doth run,
   They shall find things, they'd think, or wish, were done;
They are so natural follies, but so shown,
   As even the doers may see, and yet not own.

Act I, Scene i

[Enter] FACE, SUBTLE, DOL COMMON

FACE
  Believ't, I will.
SUBTLE   Thy worst. I fart at thee.
DOL
  Ha' you your wits? Why gentlemen! For love‒
FACE
  Sirrah, I'll strip you‒
SUBTLE   What to do? Lick figs
  Out at my‒
FACE   Rogue, rogue, out of all your sleights.
DOL
  Nay, look ye! Sovereign, General, are you madmen?   5
SUBTLE
  O, let the wild sheep loose. I'll gum your silks
  With good strong water, an' you come.
DOL   Will you have
  The neighbours hear you? Will you betray all?
  Hark, I hear somebody.
FACE   Sirrah‒
SUBTLE   I shall mar
  All that the tailor has made, if you approach.   10
FACE
  You most notorious whelp, you insolent slave
  Dare you do this?
SUBTLE   Yes faith, yes faith.
FACE   Why! Who
  Am I, my mongrel? Who am I?
SUBTLE   I'll tell you,
  Since you know not yourself‒
FACE   Speak lower, rogue.

---

  1 *Thy worst* Do your worst
  4 *out of all your sleights* Cease all your trickery
 10 *All that the tailor has made* (from the proverb) The apparel that
    makes you the man you are

---

  3 *Lick figs.* The uncompleted allusion is to an obscene story in Rabelais,
    Pantagruel, iv. xlv.
  6 *I'll gum your silks* &c. Subtle is holding a vessel containing some
    chemical preparation, and in lines 8–12 Face is prevented from attacking
    him only by fear of the chemical.

SUBTLE

Yes. You were once (time's not long past) the good,   15
Honest, plain, livery-three-pound-thrum; that kept
Your master's worship's house, here, in the Friars,
For the vacations—

FACE   Will you be so loud?

SUBTLE

Since, by my means, translated Suburb-Captain.

FACE

By your means, Doctor Dog?

SUBTLE   Within man's memory   20
All this, I speak of.

FACE   Why, I pray you, have I
Been countenanced by you? Or you, by me?
Do but collect, sir, where I met you first.

SUBTLE

I do not hear well.

FACE   Not of this, I think it.
But I shall put you in mind, sir, at Pie Corner,   25
Taking your meal of steam in, from cooks' stalls,
Where, like the Father of Hunger, you did walk
Piteously costive, with your pinched-horn-nose,
And your complexion, of the Roman wash,
Stuck full of black, and melancholic worms,   30
Like powder corns, shot, at th'artillery-yard.

SUBTLE

I wish, you could advance your voice, a little.

FACE

When you went pinned up, in the several rags,
You'd raked, and picked from dunghills, before day,

17 *Friars* Blackfriars
18 *vacations* between court terms
22 *countenanced* favoured, supported
23 *collect* recollect
24 *hear well* (bene audire) perhaps punningly
25 *Pie Corner* near Smithfield; name from a noted Inn
27 *Father of Hunger* glancing allusions to Catullus (xxi & xxiii)
28 *costive* constipated
29 *Roman wash* swarthy; hint of lotion for skin disease
31 *powder corns* grains of powder; *artillery-yard* a public place for
    arms practice
32 *advance your voice* speak louder
34 *You'd* ed. (Yo'had F.Q.)

16 *livery-three-pound-thrum.* Shabby, poorly paid servant. 'Livery' is the
servant's uniform, 'three-pound' a sneer at Face's annual wage, and
'thrum' the loose end of a weaver's warp used for tufts of coarse yarn.

Your feet in mouldy slippers, for your kibes, 35
A felt of rug, and a thin threaden cloak,
That scare would cover your no-buttocks—

SUBTLE So, sir!

FACE

When all your alchemy, and your algebra,
Your minerals, vegetals, and animals,
Your conjuring, cozening, and your dozen of trades, 40
Could not relieve your corps, with so much linen
Would make you tinder, but to see a fire;
I ga' you countenance, credit for your coals,
Your stills, your glasses, your materials,
Built you a furnace, drew you customers, 45
Advanced all your black arts; lent you, beside,
A house to practise in—

SUBTLE Your master's house?

FACE

Where you have studied the more thriving skill
Of bawdry, since.

SUBTLE Yes, in your master's house.
You, and the rats, here, kept possession. 50
Make it not strange. I know, you're one, could keep
The buttery-hatch still locked, and save the chippings,
Sell the dole-beer to aqua-vitae-men,
The which, together with your Christmas vails,
At post and pair, your letting out of counters, 55
Made you a pretty stock, some twenty marks,
And gave you credit, to converse with cobwebs,
Here, since your mistress' death hath broke up house.

FACE

You might talk softlier, rascal.

SUBTLE No, you scarab,
I'll thunder you, in pieces. I will teach you 60
How to beware, to tempt a Fury again
That carries tempest in his hand, and voice.

36 *felt of rug* coarse hat
41 *corps* body
51 *Make it not strange* don't affect bewilderment, make mysteries
53 *dole-beer* meant for distribution to the poor; *aqua-vitae-men* dealers in spirits
54 *vails* tips
55 *post and pair* a card game; *counters* to facilitate gambling
59 *scarab* beetle, dung-fly

---

53 *Sell the dole-beer* &c. Cf. *The Devil is an Ass*, II.i, 4–7.
58 *your mistress' death.* Lovewit, Face's master, is thus a widower, and available for sudden marriage in Act V.

FACE

The place has made you valiant.

SUBTLE   No, your clothes.

Thou vermin, have I ta'en thee, out of dung,
So poor, so wretched, when no living thing   65
Would keep thee company, but a spider, or worse?
Raised thee from brooms, and dust, and watering-pots?
Sublimed thee, and exalted thee, and fixed thee
I'the third region, called our state of grace?
Wrought thee to spirit, to quintessence, with pains   70
Would twice have won me the philosopher's work?
Put thee in words, and fashion? Made thee fit
For more than ordinary fellowships?
Given thee thy oaths, thy quarrelling dimensions?
Thy rules, to cheat at horse-race, cock-pit, cards,   75
Dice, or whatever gallant tincture, else?
Made thee a second, in mine own great art?
And have I this for thank? Do you rebel?
Do you fly out, i' the projection?
Would you be gone, now?

DOL   Gentlemen, what mean you?   80
Will you mar all?

SUBTLE   Slave, thou hadst had no name—

DOL

Will you undo yourselves, with civil war?

SUBTLE

Never been known, past *equi clibanum*,
The heat of horse-dung, under ground, in cellars,
Or an ale-house, darker than deaf John's: been lost   85
To all mankind, but laundresses, and tapsters,
Had not I been.

DOL   Do you know who hears you, Sovereign?

FACE

Sirrah—

---

71 *philosopher's work* elixir
73 *fellowships* partnership in companies
74 *oaths* part of the alchemical mystique; *quarrelling dimensions*
   how far to take a quarrel (*cf.* II.vi, 65 ff.)
76 *tincture* used in alchemical sense
85 *deaf John's* now unknown (HS)

---

79 *Do you fly out* &c. Do you explode at the moment of perfection? – a
   disaster incident to alchemists.
83 *equi clibanum*. 'the furnace of the horse'. The heat of horse-dung was
   a moderate heat, used in alchemical processes.

DOL   Nay, General, I thought you were civil—

FACE
    I shall turn desperate, if you grow thus loud.

SUBTLE
    And hang thyself, I care not.

FACE   Hang thee, collier,   90
    And all thy pots, and pans, in picture I will,
    Since thou hast moved me—

DOL   (O, this'll o'erthrow all.)

FACE
    Write thee up bawd, in Paul's; have all thy tricks
    Of cozening with a hollow coal, dust, scrapings,
    Searching for things lost, with a sieve, and shears,   95
    Erecting figures, in your rows of houses,
    And taking in of shadows, with a glass,
    Told in red letters: and a face, cut for thee,
    Worse than Gamaliel Ratsey's.

DOL   Are you sound?
    Ha' you your senses, masters?

FACE   I will have   100
    A book, but barely reckoning thy impostures,
    Shall prove a true philosopher's stone, to printers.

90 *collier* cheat (by inference)
91 *in picture* for public exposure
93 *in Paul's* at St. Paul's – a resort favoured by cheats and criminals
96 *Erecting figures* plotting position of planets; *houses* signs of zodiac
97 *glass* a crystal or beryl
98 *red letters* used to emphasize key passages in pamphlets; *cut for thee* drawn to represent you
99 *Gamaliel Ratsey's* highwayman publicized in pamphlets; *sound* sane
102 quintessential truth, and a means of enrichment

93–97 *have all ... glass.* The hollow coal trick involved secreting silver filings in a piece of burnt wood, and then, miraculously, 'extracting' the silver. See Chaucer, *Canon's Yeoman's Tale.* The sieve and shears were traditional instruments for discovering thieves. Herford and Simpson quote Grose, *A Provincial Glossary,* 1811, p. 118:
> To discover a thief by the sieve and shears: Stick the points of the shears in the wood of the sieve, and let two persons support it, balanced upright, with their two fingers: then read a certain chapter of the Bible, and afterwards ask St. Peter and St. Paul if A. or B. is the thief, naming all the persons you suspect. On naming the real thief the sieve will turn suddenly round about.

'Erecting figures' in the casting of horoscopes was an astrologer's art, but astrology and alchemy were often closely connected. The 'shadows' in the glass were reputedly angels, who answered questions which had to be put to them by a virgin of pure life. Dr. Dee's 'glass' is in the British Museum. See also Johnstone Parr, *Tamburlaine's Malady and other essays on Astrology in Elizabethan Drama* (Alabama, 1953), 101–6.

SUBTLE
  Away, you trencher-rascal.
FACE   Out you dog-leech,
  The vomit of all prisons—
DOL   Will you be
  Your own destructions, gentlemen?
FACE   Still spewed out   105
  For lying too heavy o' the basket.
SUBTLE   Cheater.
FACE
  Bawd.
SUBTLE Cow-herd.
FACE   Conjurer.
SUBTLE   Cut-purse.
FACE   Witch.
DOL   O me!
  We are ruined! Lost! Ha' you no more regard
  To your reputations? Where's your judgment? S'light,
  Have yet, some care of me, o' your republic—   110
FACE
  Away this brach. I'll bring thee, rogue, within
  The statute of sorcery, *tricesimo tertio,*
  Of Harry the Eighth: ay, and (perhaps) thy neck
  Within a noose, for laundering gold, and barbing it.
DOL
  You'll bring your head within a coxcomb, will you?   115
  She catcheth out Face his sword: and breaks Subtle's glass
  And you, sir, with your menstrue, gather it up.
  S'death, you abominable pair of stinkards,
  Leave off your barking, and grow one again,
  Or, by the light that shines, I'll cut your throats.
  I'll not be made a prey unto the marshal,   120

103 *trencher-rascal* hanger-on; *dog-leech* quack (by inference)
106 *lying too heavy o' the basket* the mean greed of prisoners who seize
    more than a share of scraps sent in (by basket)
110 *republic* joint interests; ironic usage
111 *brach* bitch
114 *laundering, barbing* 'sweating' gold or plate, mutilating coin
116 *menstrue* menstruum (for dissolving solids)
118 *grow one* be reconciled
120 *marshal* the provost-marshal

112–13 *The statute . . . of Harry the Eighth.* Passed in 1541, though a similar
    act had been passed in 1403. It forbade the multiplying of gold or
    silver, among other things, and it was confirmed by the statute of 1
    James I, c. 12, in 1604. These acts were not repealed until 1689.

For ne'er a snarling dog-bolt o' you both.
Ha' you together cozened all this while,
And all the world, and shall it now be said
You've made most courteous shift, to cozen yourselves?
You will accuse him? You will bring him in   125
Within the statute? Who shall take your word?
A whoreson, upstart, apocryphal captain,
Whom not a puritan, in Blackfriars, will trust
So much, as for a feather! And you, too,
Will give the cause, forsooth? You will insult,   130
And claim a primacy, in the divisions?
You must be chief? As if you, only, had
The powder to project with? And the work
Were not begun out of equality?
The venture tripartite? All things in common?   135
Without priority? S'death, you perpetual curs,
Fall to your couples again, and cozen kindly,
And heartily, and lovingly, as you should,
And lose not the beginning of a term,
Or, by this hand, I shall grow factious too,   140
And, take my part, and quit you.
FACE   'Tis his fault,
  He ever murmurs, and objects his pains,
  And says, the weight of all lies upon him.
SUBTLE
  Why, so it does.
DOL   How does it? Do not we
  Sustain our parts?
SUBTLE   Yes, but they are not equal.   145
DOL
  Why, if your part exceed today, I hope
  Ours may, tomorrow, match it.
SUBTLE   Ay, they may.
DOL
  May, murmuring mastiff? Ay, and do. Death on me!

121 *dog-bolt* meaning doubtful
127 *apocryphal* without authority
130 *give the cause* assume the right to lead in argument
133 *powder to project with* powder to consummate alchemy
137 *kindly* in brotherly spirit
139 *term* term of court (meaning increase of custom)
141 *quit* requite
142 *objects* objects because of his labours
148 *Death on me* Gods will Q

128 *Blackfriars.* The area was noted as a residence of Puritans, and the
    centre of the feather trade. Cf. *Bartholomew Fair*, V.v,85-6.

Help me to throttle him.
SUBTLE   Dorothy, mistress Dorothy,
  'Ods precious, I'll do anything. What do you mean?   150
DOL
  Because o' your fermentation, and cibation?
SUBTLE
  Not I, by heaven—
DOL   Your Sol, and Luna—help me.
SUBTLE
  Would I were hanged then. I'll conform myself.
DOL
  Will you, sir, do so then, and quickly: swear.
SUBTLE
  What should I swear?
DOL   To leave your faction, sir.   155
  And labour, kindly, in the common work.
SUBTLE
  Let me not breathe, if I meant ought, beside.
  I only used those speeches, as a spur
  To him.
DOL   I hope we need no spurs, sir. Do we?
FACE
  'Slid, prove today, who shall shark best.
SUBTLE   Agreed.   160
DOL
  Yes, and work close, and friendly.
SUBTLE   'Slight, the knot
  Shall grow the stronger, for this breach, with me.
DOL
  Why so, my good baboons! Shall we go make
  A sort of sober, scurvy, precise neighbours,
  (That scarce have smiled twice, since the king came in)   165
  A feast of laughter, at our follies? Rascals,
  Would run themselves from breath, to see me ride,
  Or you t'have but a hole, to thrust your heads in,
  For which you should pay ear-rent? No, agree.

152 *Sol, and Luna* gold and silver
156 *kindly* like a brother, amicably
162 *with me* (probably) where I'm concerned
164 *sort* set, clique; *precise* Puritanical
165 i.e. 1603
167 *from breath* out of breath *ride* carted,
    as a bawd
168 *a hole* pillory
169 *ear-rent* lose your ears

And may Don Provost ride a-feasting, long,   170
In his old velvet jerkin, and stained scarves
(My noble Sovereign, and worthy General)
Ere we contribute a new crewel garter
To his most worsted worship.
SUBTLE   Royal Dol!
Spoken like Claridiana, and thyself!   175
FACE
For which, at supper, thou shalt sit in triumph,
And not be styled Dol Common, but Dol Proper,
Dol Singular: the longest cut, at night,
Shall draw thee for his Dol Particular.
SUBTLE
Who's that? One rings. To the window, Dol. Pray heaven,   180
The master do not trouble us, this quarter.
FACE
O, fear not him. While there dies one, a week,
O'the plague, he's safe, from thinking toward London.
Beside, he's busy at his hop-yards, now:
I had a letter from him. If he do,   185
He'll send such word, for airing o' the house
As you shall have sufficient time, to quit it:
Though we break up a fortnight, 'tis no matter.
SUBTLE
Who is it, Dol?
DOL   A fine young quodling.
FACE   O,
My lawyer's clerk, I lighted on, last night,   190
In Holborn, at the Dagger. He would have
(I told you of him) a familiar,
To rifle with, at horses, and win cups.
DOL
O, let him in.
SUBTLE   Stay. Who shall do't?
FACE   Get you
Your robes on. I will meet him, as going out.   195

170 *Don Provost* in his role as executioner
173 *crewel* yarn (punningly)
174 *worsted* coarse yarn (punningly again)
188 *break up* dissolve partnership (temporarily)
189 *quodling* codling, 'green' boy
191 *Dagger* famous inn
192 *familiar* familiar spirit, at call
193 *rifle* gamble (raffle)

175 *Claridiana*. Heroine of the romance *The Mirror of Knighthood*.

DOL
  And what shall I do?
FACE   Not be seen, away.
  Seem you very reserved.   [*Exit* DOL]
SUBTLE   Enough.   [*Exit* SUBTLE]
FACE   God be w'you, sir.
  I pray you, let him know that I was here.
  His name is Dapper. I would gladly have stayed, but—

Act I, Scene ii

[*Enter*] DAPPER, FACE

DAPPER
  Captain, I am here.
FACE   Who's that? He's come, I think, Doctor.
  Good faith, sir, I was going away.
DAPPER   In truth,
  I am very sorry, Captain.
FACE   But I thought
  Sure, I should meet you.
DAPPER   Ay, I am very glad.
  I had a scurvy writ, or two, to make,   5
  And I had lent my watch last night, to one
  That dines, today, at the sheriff's: and so was robbed
  Of my pass-time. [*Enter* SUBTLE] Is this the cunning-man?
FACE
  This is his worship.
DAPPER   Is he a Doctor?
FACE   Yes.
DAPPER
  And ha' you broke with him, Captain?
FACE   Ay.
DAPPER   And how?   10
FACE
  Faith, he does make the matter, sir, so dainty,
  I know not what to say—
DAPPER   Not so, good Captain.
FACE
  Would I were fairly rid on't, believe me.

  9 *Doctor* in sense of high skill, learning
  10 *broke* opened up the matter
  11 *dainty* not anxious to touch it; dangerous
  13 *rid on't* quit of the matter

  6 *my watch*. Watches, at this time, were scarce and expensive. Dapper is
  boasting, or pretending, that he owns one. Cf. *Twelfth Night*, II.v.

DAPPER

    Nay, now you grieve me, sir. Why should you wish so?

    I dare assure you. I'll not be ungrateful.   15

FACE

    I cannot think you will, sir. But the law

    Is such a thing—and then, he says, Read's matter

    Falling so lately—

DAPPER   Read? He was an ass,

    And dealt, sir, with a fool.

FACE   It was a clerk, sir.

DAPPER

    A clerk?

FACE   Nay, hear me, sir, you know the law   20

    Better, I think—

DAPPER   I should, sir, and the danger.

    You know I showed the statute to you?

FACE   You did so.

DAPPER

    And will I tell, then? By this hand, of flesh,

    Would it might never write good court-hand, more,

    If I discover. What do you think of me,   25

    That I am a chouse?

FACE   What's that?

DAPPER   The Turk was, here—

    As one would say, do you think I am a Turk?

FACE

    I'll tell the Doctor so.

DAPPER   Do, good sweet Captain.

FACE

    Come, noble Doctor, pray thee, let's prevail,

    This is the gentleman, and he is no chouse.   30

SUBTLE

    Captain, I have returned you all my answer.

24 *court-hand* law-court script
25 *discover* reveal
26 *chouse* (or chiaus: slang from Turkish) cheat

---

17 *Read's matter*. Dr. Simon Read, physician, was pardoned by the King
for having on 8th November, 1607, invoked spirits to find who had stolen
£37 10s. from Toby Matthew (the 'fool' of line 19). See Rymer,
Foedera, xvi, 666.
26 *The Turk*. A Turk named Mustafa reached England towards the end of
July, 1607, saying he was an ambassador from the Sultan, though he
took no higher title than *Chāush* (messenger or herald). The Levant
merchants were obliged to entertain him, for fear of offending the
Sultan, and he was even received at Windsor. He left in November,
1607, having added a new word to the language.

I would do much, sir, for your love–but this
I neither may, nor can.

FACE   Tut, do not say so.
You deal, now, with a noble fellow, Doctor,
One that will thank you, richly, and he's no chouse: 35
Let that, sir, move you.

SUBTLE   Pray you, forbear—

FACE   He has
Four angels, here—

SUBTLE   You do me wrong, good sir.

FACE

Doctor, wherein? To tempt you, with these spirits?

SUBTLE

To tempt my art, and love, sir, to my peril.
Fore heaven, I scarce can think you are my friend,   40
That so would draw me to apparent danger.

FACE

I draw you? A horse draw you, and a halter,
You, and your flies together—

DAPPER   Nay, good Captain.

FACE

That know no difference of men.

SUBTLE   Good words, sir.

FACE

Good deeds, sir, Doctor Dogs-meat. 'Slight I bring you   45
No cheating Clim o' the Cloughs, or Claribels,
That look as big as five-and-fifty, and flush,
And spit out secrets, like hot custard—

DAPPER   Captain.

FACE

Nor any melancholic under-scribe,

37 *angels* gold coin worth over 10/–
38 *spirits* angels
42 *draw you* i.e. in a cart, to Tyburn
43 *flies* familiar demons
44 *difference* distinction (social, and between honest and fraud)
45 *Dogs-meat* carrion; Q has *dogs-mouth*, with possible sense of
  'barking at all comers'

---

46 *No cheating Clim* &c. Heroes of ballad and romance. Clim was a celebrated archer and outlaw of the North; see the *Ballad of Adam Bell*
  (Percy, *Reliques*, I.156). Sir Claribel is one of the knights contending
  for the false Florimel in *The Faerie Queene*, IV, ix. 'Cheating' is puzzl-
  ing; Herford and Simpson suggest that some contemporary thief might
  have adopted Clim's name.
47 *five-and-fifty, and flush.* A complete sequence in the same suit, an
  invincible hand in the game of Primero.

Shall tell the vicar: but, a special gentle,						50
That is the heir to forty marks, a year,
Consorts with the small poets of the time,
Is the sole hope of his old grandmother,
That knows the law, and writes you six fair hands,
Is a fine clerk, and has his cyphering perfect,					55
Will take his oath, o' the Greek Xenophon
If need be, in his pocket: and can court
His mistress, out of Ovid.

DAPPER				Nay, dear Captain.

FACE

Did you not tell me, so?

DAPPER				Yes, but I'd ha' you
Use master Doctor, with some more respect.					60

FACE

Hang him proud stag, with his broad velvet head.
But, for your sake, I'd choke, ere I would change
An article of breath, with such a puck-fist—
Come let's be gone.

SUBTLE				Pray you, le' me speak with you.

DAPPER

His worship calls you, Captain.

FACE				I am sorry,							65
I e'er embarked myself, in such a business.

DAPPER

Nay, good sir. He did call you.

FACE				Will he take, then?

SUBTLE

First, hear me—

FACE				Not a syllable, 'less you take.

SUBTLE

Pray ye, sir—

FACE				Upon no terms, but an *assumpsit*.

SUBTLE

Your humour must be law.

				He takes the money

FACE				Why now, sir, talk.							70
Now, I dare hear you with mine honour. Speak.
So may this gentleman too.

50 *vicar* vicar-general: chancellor, acting for bishop (HS)
51 *marks* worth (then) about 15/–
61 *head* i.e. hat
63 *article* punningly, to Dapper
67 *take* confirm the agreement
68 *'less* unless
69 *assumpsit* voluntary verbal promise

SUBTLE   Why, sir—
FACE   No whispering.
SUBTLE
  'Fore heaven, you do not apprehend the loss
  You do yourself, in this.
FACE   Wherein? For what?
SUBTLE
  Marry, to be so importunate for one,   75
  That, when he has it, will undo you all:
  He'll win up all the money i' the town.
FACE
  How!
SUBTLE Yes. And blow up gamester, after gamester,
  As they do crackers, in a puppet-play.
  If I do give him a familiar,   80
  Give you him all you play for; never set him:
  For he will have it.
FACE   You're mistaken, Doctor.
  Why, he does ask one but for cups, and horses,
  A rifling fly: none o' your great familiars.
DAPPER
  Yes, Captain, I would have it, for all games.   85
SUBTLE
  I told you so.
FACE   'Slight, that's a new business!
  I understood you, a tame bird, to fly
  Twice in a term, or so; on Friday nights,
  When you had left the office: for a nag,
  Of forty, or fifty shillings.
DAPPER   Ay, 'tis true, sir,   90
  But I do think, now, I shall leave the law,
  And therefore—
FACE   Why, this changes quite the case!
  D'you think, that I dare move him?
DAPPER   If you please, sir,
  All's one to him, I see.
FACE   What! For that money?
  I cannot with my conscience. Nor should you   95
  Make the request, methinks.
DAPPER   No, sir, I mean
  To add consideration.

78 *blow up* ruin, explode
81 *set* stake against
84 *rifling fly* demon for raffles
92 *therefore* – so F (Q has *therefore*. i.e. on that account)
97 *consideration* payment

FACE   Why, then, sir,
  I'll try. Say, that it were for all games, Doctor?
SUBTLE
  I say, then, not a mouth shall eat for him
  At any ordinary, but o' the score,   100
  That is a gaming mouth, conceive me.
FACE   Indeed!
SUBTLE
  He'll draw you all the treasure of the realm,
  If it be set him.
FACE   Speak you this from art?
SUBTLE
  Ay, sir, and reason too: the ground of art.
  He's o' the only best complexion,   105
  The Queen of Fairy loves.
FACE   What! Is he!
SUBTLE   Peace.
  He'll overhear you. Sir, should she but see him—
FACE
  What?
SUBTLE Do not you tell him.
FACE   Will he win at cards too?
SUBTLE
  The spirits of dead Holland, living Isaac,
  You'd swear, were in him: such a vigorous luck   110
  As cannot be resisted. 'Slight he'll put
  Six o' your gallants, to a cloak, indeed.
FACE
  A strange success, that some man shall be born to!
SUBTLE
  He hears you, man—

103 *set him* required of him (i.e. of the familiar)
105–6 i.e. favoured by supernatural powers
112 *to a cloak* strip to the cloak

99–100 *not a mouth . . . score.* i.e. at any inn he will get all the meals he
    orders on credit. An 'ordinary' was originally a meal prepared at an inn
    at a fixed price. It came to mean the inn itself.
109 *dead Holland, living Isaac.* 'John and John Isaac, surnamed Holland,
    reputed to have been the first Dutch alchemists in the first half of the
    fifteenth century' (Herford and Simpson). Their works were not
    published until the beginning of the seventeenth century, and this may
    have misled Jonson into speaking of 'living Isaac'. Several of Jonson's
    earlier editors doubted this identification, on the grounds that luck in
    gambling would not be associated with the names of two Dutch al-
    chemists. But Subtle is simply concerned to dazzle Dapper, and does
    so by this reference to recondite masters of his own art.

DAPPER   Sir, I'll not be ingrateful.
FACE
  Faith, I have a confidence in his good nature: 115
  You hear, he says, he will not be ingrateful.
SUBTLE
  Why, as you please, my venture follows yours.
FACE
  Troth, do it, Doctor. Think him trusty, and make him.
  He may make us both happy in an hour:
  Win some five thousand pound, and send us two on't.   120
DAPPER
  Believe it, and I will, sir.
FACE   And you shall, sir.
  You have heard all?
DAPPER   No, what was't? Nothing, I sir.
                    Face takes him aside
FACE
  Nothing?
DAPPER   A little, sir.
FACE   Well, a rare star
  Reigned, at your birth.
DAPPER   At mine, sir? No.
FACE   The Doctor
  Swears that you are—
SUBTLE   Nay, Captain, you'll tell all, now.   125
FACE
  Allied to the Queen of Fairy.
DAPPER   Who? That I am?
  Believe it, no such matter—
FACE   Yes, and that
  Yo' were born with a caul o' your head.
DAPPER   Who says so?
FACE   Come.
  You know it well enough, though you dissemble it.
DAPPER
  I'fac, I do not. You are mistaken.
FACE   How!   130
  Swear by your fac? And in a thing so known
  Unto the Doctor? How shall we, sir, trust you
  I' the other matter? Can we ever think,

119 *happy* rich like the Latin *beatus* (HS)
130 *fac* coy corruption of faith

128 *born with a caul.* A sign of good fortune. Cf. French *né coiffé.*

When you have won five, or six thousand pound,
You'll send us shares in't, by this rate?
DAPPER   By Jove, sir,   135
I'll win ten thousand pound, and send you half.
I'fac's no oath.
SUBTLE   No, no, he did but jest.
FACE
Go to. Go, thank the Doctor. He's your friend
To take it so.
DAPPER   I thank his worship.
FACE   So?
Another angel.
DAPPER   Must I?
FACE   Must you? 'Slight,   140
What else is thanks? Will you be trivial? Doctor,
When must he come, for his familiar?
DAPPER
Shall I not ha' it with me?
SUBTLE   O, good sir!
There must a world of ceremonies pass,
You must be bathed, and fumigated, first;   145
Besides, the Queen of Fairy does not rise,
Till it be noon.
FACE   Not, if she danced, tonight.
SUBTLE
And she must bless it.
FACE   Did you never see
Her royal Grace, yet?
DAPPER   Whom?
FACE   Your aunt of Fairy?
SUBTLE
Not, since she kissed him, in the cradle, Captain,   150
I can resolve you that.
FACE   Well, see her Grace,
Whate'er it cost you, for a thing that I know!
It will be somewhat hard to compass: but,
How ever, see her. You are made, believe it,
If you can see her. Her Grace is a lone woman,   155
And very rich, and if she take a fancy,

147 *tonight* last night

---

137 *I'fac's no oath.* A strict Puritan did not allow himself to swear at all.
His yea was yea, and his nay, nay (*Matthew*, v,34, and *James*, v,12). It
became a sign of 'respectability' to limit one's oaths, and Dapper's
coyness exemplifies his pretended status.

She will do strange things. See her, at any hand.
'Slid, she may hap to leave you all she has!
It is the Doctor's fear.

DAPPER   How will't be done, then?

FACE

Let me alone, take you no thought. Do you   160
But say to me, Captain, I'll see her Grace.

DAPPER

Captain, I'll see her Grace.

FACE   Enough.   *One knocks without*

SUBTLE   Who's there?

Anon. (Conduct him forth, by the back way)
Sir, against one o'clock, prepare yourself.
Till when you must be fasting; only, take   165
Three drops of vinegar, in, at your nose;
Two at your mouth; and one, at either ear;
Then, bathe your fingers' ends; and wash your eyes;
To sharpen your five senses; and, cry *hum*,
Thrice; and then *buz*, as often; and then, come.   170

FACE

Can you remember this?

DAPPER   I warrant you.

FACE

Well, then, away. 'Tis, but your bestowing
Some twenty nobles, 'mong her Grace's servants;
And, put on a clean shirt: you do not know
What grace her Grace may do you in clean linen. [*Exeunt*]   175

Act I, Scene iii

[Enter] SUBTLE

SUBTLE

Come in (Good wives, I pray you forbear me, now.
Troth I can do you no good, till afternoon)

[Enter DRUGGER]

What is your name, say you, Abel Drugger?

169–70 *hum, buz* noises for magic formulae
173 *nobles* coin worth about 8/6

---

1 *Good wives*. This is addressed to some women (probably imaginary)
waiting in another room, and it is one of the few moments in the play
when we are made aware of another world outside the immediate,
tight circle of the cozeners and the cozened.

DRUGGER   Yes, sir.

SUBTLE

  A seller of tobacco?

DRUGGER   Yes, sir.

SUBTLE   'Umh.

  Free of the grocers?

DRUGGER   Ay, and't please you.

SUBTLE   Well—   5

  Your business, Abel?

DRUGGER   This, and't please your worship,

  I am a young beginner, and am building

  Of a new shop, and't like your worship; just,

  At corner of a street: (here's the plot on't.)

  And I would know, by art, sir, of your worship,   10

  Which way I should make my door, by necromancy.

  And, where my shelves. And, which should be for boxes.

  And, which for pots. I would be glad to thrive, sir.

  And, I was wished to your worship, by a gentleman,

  One Captain Face, that says you know men's planets,   15

  And their good angels, and their bad.

SUBTLE   I do,

  If I do see 'em—

                    [*Enter* FACE]

FACE   What! My honest Abel?

  Thou art well met, here!

DRUGGER   Troth, sir, I was speaking,

  Just, as your worship came here, of your worship.

  I pray you, speak for me to master Doctor.   20

FACE

  He shall do anything. Doctor, do you hear?

  This is my friend, Abel, an honest fellow,

  He lets me have good tobacco, and he does not

  Sophisticate it, with sack-lees, or oil,

  Nor washes it in muscadel, and grains,   25

  5 *Free of the grocers* member of the Grocers' Company
  9 *plot* ground plan
 11 *necromancy* magic, especially divination of the future
 15 *planets* i.e. can cast horoscopes
 24 *Sophisticate* adulterate

---

  5 *the grocers.* Grocers, apothecaries, chandlers, and innkeepers all sold
    tobacco, as well as specialists like Drugger. Subtle is establishing that
    Drugger has served a proper apprenticeship.
 24 *Sophisticate.* Tobacco-curing was not widely understood in the seven-
    teenth century, and because it was transported between continents it
    frequently became too dry, or mouldy. Dry tobacco could be disguised
    (and increased in weight) by adulteration with wines or oils.

Nor buries it, in gravel, under ground,
Wrapped up in greasy leather, or pissed clouts:
But keeps it in fine lily-pots, that opened,
Smell like conserve of roses, or French beans.
He has his maple block, his silver tongs,   30
Winchester pipes, and fire of Juniper.
A neat, spruce-honest-fellow, and no gold-smith.
SUBTLE
He's a fortunate fellow, that I am sure on—
FACE
Already, sir, ha' you found it? Lo' thee Abel!
SUBTLE
And, in right way toward riches—
FACE   Sir.
SUBTLE   This summer,   35
He will be of the clothing of his company:
And, next spring, called to the scarlet. Spend what he can.
FACE
What, and so little beard?
SUBTLE   Sir, you must think,
He may have a receipt, to make hair come.
But he'll be wise, preserve his youth, and fine for't: 40
His fortune looks for him, another way.
FACE
'Slid, Doctor, how canst thou know this so soon?
I am amused, at that!
SUBTLE   By a rule, Captain,
In metoposcopy, which I do work by,
A certain star i'the forehead, which you see not.   45
Your chestnut, or your olive-coloured face

29 *French beans* broad beans
32 *gold-smith* usurer
37 *scarlet* i.e. made sheriff
40 *fine* pay the fine for refusing the office (HS)
43 *amused* set musing, puzzled
44 *metoposcopy* branch of physiognomy

---

30 *He has his maple block* &c. Drugger's shop is well equipped to teach the
   art of smoking. The maple block was for shredding the tobacco leaf, the
   tongs for holding the lighted coal, and the fire of juniper for lighting
   the pipes (juniper wood burns very slowly and steadily). For 'Winchester pipes' see *Notes and Queries*, clxxxii (1942) p.x.
45–49 *A certain . . . finger.* Herford and Simpson quote Richard Sanders,
   Physiognomie and Chiromancie, Metoposcopie, 1653: 'The colours of the
   Body, and especially of the face, denote the Humour and inclination of
   the person; . . . Those that be chestnut or olive colour are Jovialists
   and honest people, open without painting or cheating.'

Does never fail: and your long ear doth promise.
I knew't, by certain spots too, in his teeth,
And on the nail of his mercurial finger.

FACE

Which finger's that?

SUBTLE   His little finger. Look.   50
You're born upon a Wednesday?

DRUGGER   Yes, indeed, sir.

SUBTLE

The thumb, in chiromanty, we give Venus;
The forefinger to Jove; the midst, to Saturn;
The ring to Sol; the least, to Mercury:
Who was the lord, sir, of his horoscope,   55
His house of life being Libra. which foreshowed,
He should be a merchant, and should trade with balance.

FACE

Why, this is strange! Is't not, honest Nab?

SUBTLE

There is a ship now, coming from Ormus,
That shall yield him, such a commodity   60
Of drugs—this is the west, and this the south?

DRUGGER

Yes, sir.

SUBTLE   And those are your two sides?

DRUGGER   Ay, sir.

SUBTLE

Make me your door, then, south; your broad side, west:
And, on the east side of your shop, aloft,
Write *Mathlai, Tarmiel*, and *Baraborat*;   65
Upon the north part, *Rael, Velel, Thiel*.
They are the names of those mercurial spirits,
That do fright flies from boxes.

DRUGGER   Yes, sir.

SUBTLE   And
Beneath your threshold, bury me a loadstone
To draw in gallants, that wear spurs: the rest,   70

---

47 *promise* i.e. promise well
52 *chiromanty* palmistry
58 *Nab* (slang) head, head-piece

---

56 *His house of life* &c. If Libra governed the house of life, Venus ruled
Libra, and not Mercury. Subtle, trading on Drugger's ignorance, sub-
stitutes the more appropriate Mercury, the god of business men.
65 *Write Mathlai* &c. Quoted, as Gifford points out, from *Heptameron, seu
Elementa magica Pietri de Abano philosophi*, appended to Cornelius
Agrippa's *De Occulta Philosophia*, Paris? 1567?

They'll seem to follow.

FACE   That's a secret, Nab!

SUBTLE

And, on your stall, a puppet, with a vice,
And a court-fucus, to call city-dames.
You shall deal much, with minerals.

DRUGGER   Sir, I have,
At home, already—

SUBTLE   Ay, I know, you have arsenic,   75
Vitriol, sal-tartar, argaile, alkali,
Cinoper: I know all. This fellow, Captain,
Will come, in time, to be a great distiller,
And give a say (I will not say directly,
But very fair) at the philosopher's stone.   80

FACE

Why, how now, Abel! Is this true?

DRUGGER   Good Captain,
What must I give?

FACE   Nay, I'll not counsel thee.
Thou hear'st what wealth (he says, spend what thou canst)
Th'art like to come to.

DRUGGER   I would gi' him a crown.

FACE

A crown! And toward such a fortune? Heart,   85
Thou shalt rather gi' him thy shop. No gold about thee?

DRUGGER

Yes, I have a portague, I ha' kept this half year.

FACE

Out on thee, Nab; 'Slight, there was such an offer—
Shalt keep't no longer, I'll gi'it him for thee?
Doctor, Nab prays your worship, to drink this: and swears   90
He will appear more grateful, as your skill
Does raise him in the world.

DRUGGER   I would entreat
Another favour of his worship.

FACE   What is't, Nab?

DRUGGER

But, to look over, sir, my almanack,

---

71 *seem* be seen in public
72 *puppet, with a vice* doll worked by wire mechanism
73 *fucus* a cosmetic
76 *sal-tartar* carbonate of potash; *argaile* crude cream of tartar;
     alkali soda-ash (HS)
77 *Cinoper* mercuric sulphide crystals
79 *a say* trial; i.e. make an attempt
87 *portague* Portuguese gold coin, worth some £4

And cross out my ill days, that I may neither   95
Bargain, nor trust upon them.
FACE   That he shall, Nab.
Leave it, it shall be done, 'gainst afternoon.
SUBTLE
And a direction for his shelves.
FACE   Now, Nab?
Art thou well pleased, Nab?
DRUGGER   Thank, sir, both your worships.
FACE   Away.
                                        [*Exit* DRUGGER]
Why, now, you smoky persecutor of nature!   100
Now, do you see, that something's to be done,
Beside your beech-coal, and your corsive waters,
Your crosslets, crucibles, and cucurbites?
You must have stuff, brought home to you, to work on?
And, yet, you think, I am at no expense,   105
In searching out these veins, then following 'em,
Then trying 'em out. 'Fore God, my intelligence
Costs me more money, than my share oft comes to,
In these rare works.
SUBTLE   You are pleasant, sir. How now?

Act I, Scene iv

[*Enter*] DOL

SUBTLE
What says, my dainty Dolkin?
DOL   Yonder fish-wife
Will not away. And there's your giantess,
The bawd of Lambeth.
SUBTLE   Heart, I cannot speak with 'em.

---

102 *corsive* corrosive
103 *crosslets* melting-pots; *cucurbites* retorts
107 *intelligence* i.e. what I discover, report of findings

---

100 *persecutor of nature.* Both 'follower' and 'afflicter' of nature. Alchemy
could be thought of as following nature, since it was based on the pre-
mise that all metals would have been gold if they could (cf. I.iv, 25–8),
and the alchemist's 'art' is only perfecting the natural process. Yet he
could also be seen as an 'afflicter' of metals, torturing them through
furnace, alembic and still.

DOL

    Not, afore night, I have told 'em, in a voice,
    Thorough the trunk, like one of your familiars.   5
    But I have spied Sir Epicure Mammon—

SUBTLE   Where?

DOL

    Coming along, at the far end of the lane,
    Slow of his feet, but earnest of his tongue,
    To one, that's with him.

SUBTLE   Face, go you, and shift.
    Dol, you must presently make ready, too—   10

DOL

    Why, what's the matter?

SUBTLE   O, I did look for him
    With the sun's rising: marvel, he could sleep!
    This is the day, I am to perfect for him
    The *magisterium*, our great work, the stone;
    And yield it, made, into his hands: of which,   15
    He has, this month, talked, as he were possessed.
    And, now, he's dealing pieces on't, away.
    Methinks, I see him, entering ordinaries,
    Dispensing for the pox; and plaguey-houses,
    Reaching his dose; walking Moorfields for lepers;   20
    And offering citizens' wives pomander-bracelets,
    As his preservative, made of the elixir;
    Searching the spittle, to make old bawds young;
    And the highways, for beggars, to make rich:
    I see no end of his labours. He will make   25
    Nature ashamed, of her long sleep: when art,
    Who's but a step-dame, shall do more, than she,
    In her best love to mankind, ever could.
    If his dream last, he'll turn the age, to gold.   [*Exeunt*]

---

  5 *trunk* tube
  9 *shift* change uniform
 20 *Reaching* extending, offering
 21 *pomander-bracelets* i.e. as talismans
 23 *spittle* hospital

Act II, Scene i

[*Enter*] MAMMON, SURLY

MAMMON

Come on, sir. Now, you set your foot on shore
In *novo orbe*; here's the rich Peru:
And there within, sir, are the golden mines,
Great Solomon's Ophir! He was sailing to't,
Three years, but we have reached it in ten months.   5
This is the day, wherein, to all my friends,
I will pronounce the happy word, be rich.
This day, you shall be *spectatissimi*.
You shall no more deal with the hollow die,
Or the frail card. No more be at charge of keeping   10
The livery-punk, for the young heir, that must
Seal, at all hours, in his shirt. No more
If he deny, ha' him beaten to't, as he is
That brings him the commodity. No more
Shall thirst of satin, or the covetous hunger   15
Of velvet entrails, for a rude-spun cloak,
To be displayed at Madam Augusta's, make
The sons of sword, and hazard fall before
The golden calf, and on their knees, whole nights,
Commit idolatry with wine, and trumpets: 20
Or go a-feasting, after drum and ensign.

8 *spectatissimi* most honoured
9 *hollow die* (plural dice) leaded dice
10 *frail card* prepared for cheating
16 *entrails* i.e. lining
17 *Madam Augusta's* mistress of a brothel
18 *of sword, and hazard* fighting men and gamblers (*cf.* Face)

1-5 *Now, you set your foot* &c. Pizarro conquered Peru in 1532, and its
name had become a symbol for boundless wealth. Solomon was believed
to have had the philosopher's stone (II.ii, 36) and to have made gold
with it in far-away Ophir, because he could not trust his courtiers with
the secret. Mammon's speech takes some of its impetus from the
account of Solomon's wealth, 1 *Kings*, x.
10-14 *No more* &c. This passage describes, obliquely, the 'commodity'
swindle, in which a borrower was compelled to take part or all of his
loan in merchandise, and realize what he could by the resale of it. The
goods were usually of some quite unsaleable nature. Cf. III.iv, 90. In
Middleton's *Michaelmas Term* Quomodo, the moneylender, sends one
of his servants to buy back the commodity at far less than it cost his
victim. Here, the 'livery-punk' is a woman employed to persuade the
young heir who is too wary to sign the mortgages in cold blood to do so
in the heat of passion.

No more of this. You shall start up young viceroys,
And have your punks, and punketees, my Surly.
And unto thee, I speak it first, be rich.
Where is my Subtle, there? Within ho?

FACE   Sir.   *Within*   25
He'll come to you, by and by.

MAMMON   That's his fire-drake,
His lungs, his Zephyrus, he that puffs his coals,
Till he firk nature up, in her own centre.
You are not faithful, sir. This night, I'll change
All, that is metal, in thy house, to gold.   30
And, early in the morning, will I send
To all the plumbers, and the pewterers,
And buy their tin, and lead up: and to Lothbury,
For all the copper.

SURLY   What, and turn that too?

MAMMON
Yes, and I'll purchase Devonshire, and Cornwall,   35
And make them perfect Indies! You admire now?

SURLY
No faith.

MAMMON   But when you see th'effects of the great medicine!
Of which one part projected on a hundred
Of Mercury, or Venus, or the moon,
Shall turn it, to as many of the sun;   40
Nay, to a thousand, so *ad infinitum:*
You will believe me.

SURLY   Yes, when I see't, I will.
But, if my eyes do cozen me so (and I
Giving 'em no occasion) sure, I'll have
A whore, shall piss 'em out, next day.

MAMMON   Ha! Why?   45
Do you think, I fable with you? I assure you,
He that has once the flower of the sun,
The perfect ruby, which we call elixir,
Not only can do that, but by its virtue,

23 *punketees* slang term – 'punquettes'
28 *firk* drive, force (also, cheat)
36 *perfect Indies* i.e. change their tin and copper to gold
49 *virtue* power

33 *Lothbury.* An area noted for its foundries. See Stow, *A Survey of London*, 1598, p. 220.
37–40 *But when . . . sun.* Cf. Chaucer, *Canon's Yeoman's Tale*, 272–6.

Can confer honour, love, respect, long life,   50
Give safety, valour: yea, and victory,
To whom he will. In eight, and twenty days,
I'll make an old man, of fourscore, a child.

SURLY

No doubt, he's that already.

MAMMON   Nay, I mean,
Restore his years, renew him, like an eagle,   55
To the fifth age; make him get sons, and daughters,
Young giants; as our philosophers have done
(The ancient patriarchs afore the flood)
But taking, once a week, on a knive's point,
The quantity of a grain of mustard, of it: 60
Become stout Marses, and beget young Cupids.

SURLY

The decayed Vestals of Pict-Hatch would thank you,
That keep the fire alive, there.

MAMMON   'Tis the secret
Of nature, naturized 'gainst all infections,
Cures all diseases, coming of all causes,   65
A month's grief, in a day; a year's, in twelve:
And, of what age soever, in a month.
Past all the doses, of your drugging Doctors.
I'll undertake, withal, to fright the plague
Out o' the kingdom, in three months.

SURLY   And I'll   70
Be bound the players shall sing your praises, then,
Without their poets.

MAMMON   Sir, I'll do't. Meantime,
I'll give away so much, unto my man,
Shall serve th' whole city, with preservative,
Weekly, each house his dose, and at the rate—   75

57 *philosophers* alchemists (here)
62 *Pict-Hatch* near Clerkenwell; resort of prostitutes
64 *naturized* naturata, as distinct from naturans
74 *preservative* i.e. medicinal

---

55 *like an eagle*. This refers to the idea that every ten years the eagle soars
     into the 'fiery region', then plunges into the sea, where, moulting its
     feathers, it acquires new life. But there is also an unmistakable allusion
     to *Psalms*, ciii, 5, and a suitably blasphemous irony.
58 The patriarchs, from Adam to Noah, were believed to have understood
     alchemy among other mysteries. Their great ages, as recorded in
     Genesis, were taken as proof that they possessed the philosopher's stone.
71 *the players shall sing your praises*. For fear of spreading infection the
     London theatres were closed when the number of cases of plague
     reached a statutory limit, variously given as thirty and forty.

SURLY
  As he that built the waterwork, does with water?
MAMMON
  You are incredulous.
SURLY   Faith, I have a humour,
  I would not willingly be gulled. Your stone
  Cannot transmute me.
MAMMON   Pertinax, Surly,
  Will you believe antiquity? Records?   80
  I'll show you a book, where Moses, and his sister,
  And Solomon have written, of the art;
  Ay, and a treatise penned by Adam.
SURLY   How!
MAMMON
  O' the philosopher's stone, and in High Dutch.
SURLY
  Did Adam write, sir, in High Dutch?
MAMMON   He did: 85
  Which proves it was the primitive tongue.
SURLY   What paper?
MAMMON
  On cedar board.
SURLY   O that, indeed (they say)
  Will last 'gainst worms.
MAMMON   'Tis like your Irish wood,
  'Gainst cobwebs. I have a piece of Jason's fleece, too,
  Which was no other, than a book of alchemy,   90
  Writ in large sheepskin, a good fat ram-vellum.
  Such was Pythagoras' thigh, Pandora's tub;
  And, all that fable of Medea's charms,
  The manner of our work: the bulls, our furnace,

77 *humour* i.e. it is my nature   79 *Pertinax* pertinacity
91 *ram-vellum* parchment of ram's hide

---

76 *waterwork.* Waterworks supplying different parts of London with
   water from the Thames were built in 1582 and 1594. See Stow, *A
   Survey of London*, 1598, p. 18.
81–83 *I'll show . . . Adam.* Writers on alchemy frequently claimed Adam,
   Moses, Miriam and Solomon as masters in that art. Many of the works
   attributed to them are collected in J. A. Fabricius, *Codex Pseudepi-
   graphus Veteris Testamenti*, 1713.
85 *High Dutch.* 'Ioannes Goropius Becanus, a man very learned . . . letted
   not to maintaine it [the German language] to bee the first and moste
   ancient language of the world; yea the same that Adam spake in Paradise.' Richard Verstegan, *A Restitution of Decayed Intelligence*, 1605,
   p. 190.
89–100 *I have a piece . . . fixed.* All these interpretations could be found in a
   book like Martin Delrio, *Disquisitiones Magicae*, 1599.

Still breathing fire; our argent-vive, the dragon: 95
The dragon's teeth, mercury sublimate,
That keeps the whiteness, hardness, and the biting;
And they are gathered, into Jason's helm,
(Th' alembic) and then sowed in Mars his field,
And, thence, sublimed so often, till they are fixed.   100
Both this, th' Hesperian garden, Cadmus' story,
Jove's shower, the boon of Midas, Argus' eyes,
Boccace his Demogorgon, thousands more,
All abstract riddles of our stone. How now?

Act II, Scene ii

[*Enter*] FACE

MAMMON
Do we succeed? Is our day come? And holds it?
FACE
The evening will set red, upon you, sir;
You have colour for it, crimson: the red ferment
Has done his office. Three hours hence, prepare you
To see projection.
MAMMON   Pertinax, my Surly,   5
Again, I say to thee, aloud: be rich.
This day, thou shalt have ingots: and, tomorrow,
Give lords th'affront. Is it, my Zephyrus, right?
Blushes the bolt's head?
FACE   Like a wench with child, sir,
That were, but now, discovered to her master.   10
MAMMON
Excellent witty Lungs! My only care is,
Where to get stuff, enough now, to project on,
This town will not half serve me.
FACE   No, sir? Buy
The covering off o' churches.
MAMMON   That's true.
FACE   Yes.
Let 'em stand bare, as do their auditory.   15
Or cap 'em, new, with shingles.
MAMMON   No, good thatch:
Thatch will lie light upo' the rafters, Lungs.

95 *argent-vive* mercury   99 *alembic* distilling apparatus
102 *Jove's shower* i.e. the Danae   3 *crimson cf.* II.i, 48
5 *projection* last stage in alchemy   8 *affront* look in the eye
9 *bolt's head* globular flask

101–4 *th' Hesperian garden* &c. From Robertus Vallensis, *De Veritate et
    Antiquitate Artis Chemiae*, Paris, 1561.

Lungs, I will manumit thee, from the furnace;
I will restore thee thy complexion, Puff,
Lost in the embers; and repair this brain,   20
Hurt wi' the fume o' the metals.

FACE   I have blown, sir,
Hard, for your worship; thrown by many a coal,
When 'twas not beech; weighed those I put in, just,
To keep your heat, still even; these bleared eyes
Have waked, to read your several colours, sir,   25
Of the pale citron, the green lion, the crow,
The peacock's tail, the plumed swan.

MAMMON   And, lastly,
Thou hast descried the flower, the *sanguis agni?*

FACE
Yes, sir.

MAMMON Where's master?

FACE   At's prayers, sir, he,
Good man, he's doing his devotions,   30
For the success.

MAMMON   Lungs, I will set a period,
To all thy labours: thou shalt be the master
Of my seraglio.

FACE   Good, sir.

MAMMON   But do you hear?
I'll geld you, Lungs.

FACE   Yes, sir.

MAMMON   For I do mean
To have a list of wives, and concubines,   35
Equal with Solomon; who had the stone
Alike, with me: and I will make me, a back
With the elixir, that shall be as tough
As Hercules, to encounter fifty a night.
Th'art sure, thou saw'st it blood?

FACE   Both blood, and spirit, sir.   40

18 *manumit* release   31 *period* stop, end
40 *blood cf.* line 28

---

23 *not beech.* It was crucial that the alchemist's fire should be made of
beech, which was thought to be the best wood for maintaining a steady
heat.

25 *several colours.* These colours showed the various degrees of fermentation. There seems to have been no fixed scale common to all alchemists,
but black (the crow) and green (the lion) were matters for congratulation
when achieved, while white (the swan) and yellow (citron) were ascend-
ing stages towards red, the colour of projection. Jonson's audience
would have been mystified by all these terms except *sanguis agni*, the
associations of which would have been quite clear.

MAMMON

I will have all my beds, blown up; not stuffed:
Down is too hard. And then, mine oval room,
Filled with such pictures, as Tiberius took
From Elephantis: and dull Aretine
But coldly imitated. Then, my glasses,   45
Cut in more subtle angles, to disperse,
And multiply the figures, as I walk
Naked between my succubae. My mists
I'll have of perfume, vapoured 'bout the room,
To lose ourselves in; and my baths, like pits   50
To fall into: from whence, we will come forth,
And roll us dry in gossamer, and roses.
(Is it arrived at ruby?)–Where I spy
A wealthy citizen, or rich lawyer,
Have a sublimed pure wife, unto that fellow   55
I'll send a thousand pound, to be my cuckold.

FACE

And I shall carry it?

MAMMON   No. I'll ha' no bawds,
But fathers, and mothers. They will do it best.
Best of all others. And, my flatterers
Shall be the pure, and gravest of Divines,   60
That I can get for money. My mere fools,
Eloquent burgesses, and then my poets
The same that writ so subtly of the fart,

---

48 *succubae* both female demon, and harlot – double sense intended
55 *sublimed* sublimated (alchemical), refined (figuratively)
57 *carry it?* so F (Q carry it.)
62 *burgesses* members of Parliament

---

41 *beds, blown up.* Lampridius, *Heliogabalus*, 19 and 25.
43 *Tiberius* &c. Suetonius, *Tiberius*, 43. Elephantis was a Roman author, known only from the references in Suetonius and Martial (*Epigrams*, XII, xliii).
44 *Aretine.* Pietro Aretino (1492–1556), playwright and journalist. The reference is to the sixteen obscene designs by Giulio Romano engraved by Raimondi, for which Aretino wrote sixteen *Sonnetti lussuriosi*, 1523. Cf. *Volpone*, III.iv, 96.
45 See Seneca, *Naturales Quaestiones*, I,xvi.
48 *mists.* Suetonius, *Nero*, xxxi.
58 *fathers, and mothers.* Juvenal, *Satires*, x, 304–6.
63 *the fart.* One of the most popular pieces in seventeenth century commonplace books. It is headed 'A discussion in the House of Commons on the peculiar manner in which Henry Ludlow said "noe" to a message brought by the Serjeant from the Lords' in MS. Ashmole 36-7, f.131, and dated 1607 in MS. Harley 5191, f.17. Versions were later printed in the miscellanies: see Mennis and Smith, *Musarum Deliciae*, 1656.

Whom I will entertain, still, for that subject.
The few, that would give out themselves, to be   65
Court, and town stallions, and, each-where, belie
Ladies, who are known most innocent, for them;
Those will I beg, to make me eunuchs of:
And they shall fan me with ten ostrich tails
Apiece, made in a plume, to gather wind.   70
We will be brave, Puff, now we ha' the medicine.
My meat, shall all come in, in Indian shells,
Dishes of agate, set in gold, and studded,
With emeralds, sapphires, hyacinths, and rubies.
The tongues of carps, dormice, and camels' heels,   75
Boiled i' the spirit of Sol, and dissolved pearl,
(Apicius' diet, 'gainst the epilepsy)
And I will eat these broths, with spoons of amber,
Headed with diamond, and carbuncle.
My footboy shall eat pheasants, calvered salmons,   80
Knots, godwits, lampreys: I myself will have
The beards of barbels, served, instead of salads;
Oiled mushrooms; and the swelling unctuous paps
Of a fat pregnant sow, newly cut off,
Dressed with an exquisite, and poignant sauce;   85
For which, I'll say unto my cook, there's gold,
Go forth, and be a knight.
FACE   Sir, I'll go look
A little, how it heightens.   [*Exit* FACE]
MAMMON   Do. My shirts
I'll have of taffeta-sarsnet, soft, and light
As cobwebs; and for all my other raiment   90
It shall be such, as might provoke the Persian;
Were he to teach the world riot, anew.

66 *belie* slander (to sustain the proposed reputation)
74 *hyacinths* species of gem
76 *Sol* i.e. gold
77 *Apicius'* a Roman gourmand
80 *calvered* carved while still alive
89 *taffeta-sarsnet* (or sarcenet) fine, soft silk

---

75 *camels' heels*. Lampridius, *Heliogabalus*, 20.
83 *unctuous paps* &c. Herford and Simpson quote Holland's translation of
Pliny (1601): 'sows were killed even upon the point of their farrowing,
and being readie to Pig [as our monstrous gluttons doe nowadaies,
because they would have the teats soft, tender, and full of milke].' The
air of degenerate luxury in Mammon's speeches is created for the
most part by allusion to the excesses of Roman emperors. Jonson's
judgement is the same as Gibbon's.

My gloves of fishes', and birds' skins, perfumed
With gums of paradise, and eastern air—
SURLY
And do you think to have the stone, with this?   95
MAMMON
No, I do think, t' have all this, with the stone.
SURLY
Why, I have heard, he must be *homo frugi*,
A pious, holy, and religious man,
One free from mortal sin, a very virgin.
MAMMON
That makes it, sir, he is so. But I buy it.   100
My venture brings it me. He, honest wretch,
A notable, superstitious, good soul,
Has worn his knees bare, and his slippers bald,
With prayer, and fasting for it: and, sir, let him
Do it alone, for me, still. Here he comes,   105
Not a profane word, afore him: 'tis poison.

Act II, Scene iii

[*Enter*] SUBTLE

MAMMON
Good morrow, Father.
SUBTLE   Gentle son, good morrow,
And, to your friend, there. What is he, is with you?
MAMMON
An heretic, that I did bring along,
In hope, sir, to convert him.
SUBTLE   Son, I doubt
You're covetous, that thus you meet your time   5
I' the just point: prevent your day, at morning.
This argues something, worthy of a fear
Of importune, and carnal appetite.
Take heed, you do not cause the blessing leave you,
With your ungoverned haste. I should be sorry,   10
To see my labours, now, e'en at perfection,
Got by long watching, and large patience,

93 i.e. cheverel or silk   100 *That makes* He that makes
101 *venture* financial investment   105 *alone* only
5 *meet your time* prove so punctual   6 *prevent* anticipate
8 *importune* importunate

97 *homo frugi*. The necessity of piety and austerity of life in the would-be
alchemist was insisted upon by all who taught the art.

Not prosper, where my love, and zeal hath placed 'em.
Which (heaven I call to witness, with yourself,
To whom, I have poured my thoughts) in all my ends,   15
Have looked no way, but unto public good,
To pious uses, and dear charity,
Now grown a prodigy with men. Wherein
If you, my son, should now prevaricate,
And, to your own particular lusts, employ   20
So great, and catholic a bliss: be sure,
A curse will follow, yea, and overtake
Your subtle, and most secret ways.

MAMMON   I know, sir,
You shall not need to fear me. I but come,
To ha' you confute this gentleman.

SURLY   Who is,   25
Indeed, sir, somewhat costive of belief
Toward your stone: would not be gulled.

SUBTLE   Well, son,
All that I can convince him in, is this,
The work is done: bright Sol is in his robe.
We have a medicine of the triple soul,   30
The glorified spirit. Thanks be to heaven,
And make us worthy of it. Eulenspiegel.

                          [*Enter* FACE]

FACE
Anon, sir.

SUBTLE   Look well to the register,
And let your heat, still, lessen by degrees,
To the aludels.

FACE   Yes, sir.

SUBTLE   Did you look   35
O' the bolt's head yet?

19 *prevaricate* take a crooked path
21 *catholic* universal
26 *costive* (figuratively) reticent
32 *Eulenspiegel* (owlglass) folklore name for a jesting knave
33 *register* damper
35 *aludels* pots, open at both ends (HS)

30–31 *the triple soul, The glorified spirit.* i.e. the elixir. Norton, in his
   Ordinall (ed. Ashmole, 1652) speaks of a 'treble Spirit', vital, natural
   and animal, by which the soul was knit to the body:

         Therefore in our worke as Auctors teach us,
         There must be *Corpus, Anima & Spiritus.*

FACE   Which, on D, sir?
SUBTLE   Ay.
  What's the complexion?
FACE   Whitish.
SUBTLE   Infuse vinegar,
  To draw his volatile substance, and his tincture:
  And let the water in glass E be filtered,
  And put into the gripe's egg. Lute him well;   40
  And leave him closed in *balneo*.
FACE   I will, sir.
SURLY
  What a brave language here is? Next to canting?
SUBTLE
  I have another work; you never saw, son,
  That, three days since, passed the philosopher's wheel,
  In the lent heat of Athanor; and's become   45
  Sulphur o' nature.
MAMMON   But 'tis for me?
SUBTLE   What need you?
  You have enough, in that is, perfect.
MAMMON   O, but—
SUBTLE
  Why, this is covetise!
MAMMON   No, I assure you,
  I shall employ it all, in pious uses,
  Founding of colleges, and grammar schools,   50
  Marrying young virgins, building hospitals,
  And now, and then, a church.
SUBTLE   How now?
FACE   Sir, please you,
  Shall I not change the filter?
SUBTLE   Marry, yes.
  And bring me the complexion of glass B.   [*Exit* FACE]
MAMMON
  Ha' you another?

---

40 *gripe's egg* pot shaped like griffin's egg;
   Lute make clay covering
41 *balneo* sand-bath or water-bath for gradual heating
42 *canting* thieves' jargon; possibly also puritans'
44 *philosopher's wheel* alchemical cycle
45 *lent heat* (Latin) slow fire
48 *covetise* covetousness

---

36 *on D   sir?* Several different furnaces are supposed to be operating in the
   adjoining room, distinguished by different letters.

SUBTLE   Yes, son, were I assured   55
  Your piety were firm, we would not want
  The means to glorify it. But I hope the best:
  I mean to tinct C in sand-heat, tomorrow,
  And give him imbibition.
MAMMON   Of white oil?
SUBTLE
  No, sir, of red. F is come over the helm too,   60
  I thank my Maker, in S. Mary's bath,
  And shows *lac virginis*. Blessed be heaven.
  I sent you of his faeces there, calcined.
  Out of that calx, I ha' won the salt of mercury.
MAMMON
  By pouring on your rectified water?   65
SUBTLE
  Yes, and reverberating in Athanor.

[Enter FACE]

  How now? What colour says it?
FACE   The ground black, sir.
MAMMON
  That's your crow's head?
SURLY   Your cockscomb's, is't not?
SUBTLE
  No, 'tis not perfect, would it were the crow.
  That work wants something.
SURLY   (O, I looked for this.   70
  The hay is a-pitching.)
SUBTLE   Are you sure, you loosed 'em
  I' their own menstrue?
FACE   Yes, sir, and then married 'em,
  And put 'em in a bolt's head, nipped to digestion,
  According as you bade me; when I set
  The liquor of Mars to circulation,   75
  In the same heat.
SUBTLE   The process, then, was right.

---

59 *imbibition* soaking   60 *helm* cap of a retort
61 *Mary's bath* heat-bath
63 *sent you* (used impersonally)
   faeces sediment
64 *calx* thoroughly burnt powder; *salt* oxide
66 *reverberating* reflected heat   67 *ground* putrefying
68 *crow's head* symbolizing total calcination
71 *hay* netted snare for rabbits
73 *digestion* (chemically) substance exposed to liquid, heated
75 *liquor of Mars* molten iron

FACE

    Yes, by the token, sir, the retort broke,

    And what was saved, was put into the pelican,

    And signed with Hermes' seal.

SUBTLE   I think 'twas so.

    We should have a new amalgama.

SURLY   O, this ferret   80

    Is rank as any pole-cat.

SUBTLE   But I care not.

    Let him e'en die; we have enough beside,

    In embrion. H has his white shirt on?

FACE   Yes, sir,

    He's ripe for inceration: he stands warm,

    In his ash-fire. I would not, you should let   85

    Any die now, if I might counsel, sir,

    For luck's sake to the rest. It is not good.

MAMMON

    He says right.

SURLY   Ay, are you bolted?

FACE   Nay, I know't, sir,

    I have seen th' ill fortune. What is some three ounces

    Of fresh materials?

MAMMON   Is't no more?

FACE   No more, sir,   90

    Of gold, t'amalgam, with some six of mercury.

MAMMON

    Away, here's money. What will serve?

FACE   Ask him, sir.

MAMMON

    How much?

SUBTLE   Give him nine pound: you may gi' him ten.

SURLY

    Yes, twenty, and be cozened, do.

MAMMON   There 'tis.

SUBTLE

    This needs not. But that you will have it, so,   95

    To see conclusions of all. For two

    Of our inferior works, are at fixation.

---

78 *pelican* vessel so shaped   79 i.e. hermetically sealed

80 *amalgama* mixture of metals with mercury; *ferret*
(see line 71) to drive the rabbit out and (line 88) 'bolt' it

83 *embrion* (chemically) metal still in combination

84 *inceration* making into moist wax   94 *cozened* cheated

97 *fixation* reduction of the volatile to permanent form, conversion
(of mercury) into solid

A third is in ascension. Go your ways.
Ha' you set the oil of Luna in kemia?

FACE
Yes, sir.

SUBTLE   And the philosopher's vinegar?

FACE   Ay.   [*Exit* FACE]   100

SURLY
We shall have a salad.

MAMMON   When do you make projection?

SUBTLE
Son, be not hasty, I exalt our medicine,
By hanging him in *balneo vaporoso*;
And giving him solution; then congeal him;
And then dissolve him; then again congeal him;   105
For look, how oft I iterate the work,
So many times, I add unto his virtue.
As, if at first, one ounce convert a hundred,
After his second loose, he'll turn a thousand;
His third solution, ten; his fourth, a hundred.   110
After his fifth, a thousand thousand ounces
Of any imperfect metal, into pure
Silver, or gold, in all examinations,
As good, as any of the natural mine.
Get you your stuff here, against afternoon,   115
Your brass, your pewter, and your andirons.

MAMMON
Not those of iron?

SUBTLE   Yes, you may bring them, too.
We'll change all metals.

SURLY   I believe you, in that.

MAMMON
Then I may send my spits?

SUBTLE   Yes, and your racks.

SURLY
And dripping pans, and pot-hangers, and hooks?   120
Shall he not?

SUBTLE   If he please.

SURLY   To be an ass.

SUBTLE
How, sir!

MAMMON   This gentleman, you must bear withal.

98 *ascension* distillation
99 *oil of Luna* white elixir; *kemia* a cucurbit (chymia)
100 *philosopher's vinegar* universal dissolvent
101 *salad* punningly also sallad, a recognized alchemical compound
109 *loose* i.e. in solution   116 *andirons* bars to support fire

I told you, he had no faith.
SURLY   And little hope, sir,
But, much less charity, should I gull myself.
SUBTLE
Why, what have you observed, sir, in our art,   125
Seems so impossible?
SURLY   But your whole work, no more.
That you should hatch gold in a furnace, sir,
As they do eggs, in Egypt!
SUBTLE   Sir, do you
Believe that eggs are hatched so?
SURLY   If I should?
SUBTLE
Why, I think that the greater miracle.   130
No egg, but differs from a chicken, more,
Than metals in themselves.
SURLY   That cannot be.
The egg's ordained by nature, to that end:
And is a chicken in *potentia*.
SUBTLE
The same we say of lead, and other metals,   135
Which would be gold, if they had time.
MAMMON   And that
Our art doth further.
SUBTLE   Ay, for 'twere absurd
To think that nature, in the earth, bred gold
Perfect, i' the instant. Something went before.
There must be remote matter.
SURLY   Ay, what is that?   140

126 *But* only   139 *Perfect* (here, and passim) complete
140 *remote* prima materia, the first matter

---

128 *eggs, in Egypt*. The Egyptians hatched eggs by incubation in an oven
heated by burning dung. See Pliny, *Natural History*, trans. Holland,
1635, x.liv.
131–76 *No egg, but differs* &c. This is the orthodox theory of alchemy, so
Subtle can afford to set it forth quite clearly. If we grant the principles (1)
the ultimate convertibility of matter from one state into another (2)
the properties of a substance are due to the existence of universal
principles in that substance (e.g. honey is sweet because it contains
some portion of that sweetness which exists apart from all sweet things)
then the argument is logical. As the egg strives to become a chicken,
so all metals strive to become gold. Subtle does no more than develop
these commonplaces, and locks up the argument by appeal to the theory
of spontaneous generation (171–6), which was widely believed at the
time. Herford and Simpson point out that the whole of this passage is
taken from Delrio, *Disquisitiones Magicae*, i.83. It is explained in detail
in Hathaway's edition of *The Alchemist*, pp. 20–23.

SUBTLE
   Marry, we say—
MAMMON   Ay, now it heats: stand Father.
   Pound him to dust—
SUBTLE   It is, of the one part,
   A humid exhalation, which we call
   Materia liquida, or the unctuous water;
   On th' other part, a certain crass, and viscous   145
   Portion of earth; both which, concorporate,
   Do make the elementary matter of gold:
   Which is not, yet, *propria materia*,
   But common to all metals, and all stones.
   For, where it is forsaken of that moisture   150
   And hath more dryness, it becomes a stone;
   Where it retains more of the humid fatness,
   It turns to sulphur, or to quicksilver:
   Who are the parents of all other metals.
   Nor can this remote matter, suddenly,   155
   Progress so from extreme, unto extreme,
   As to grow gold, and leap o'er all the means.
   Nature doth, first, beget th' imperfect; then
   Proceeds she to the perfect. Of that airy,
   And oily water, mercury is engendered;   160
   Sulphur o' the fat, and earthy part: the one
   (Which is the last) supplying the place of male,
   The other of the female, in all metals.
   Some do believe hermaphrodeity,
   That both do act, and suffer. But, these two   165
   Make the rest ductile, malleable, extensive.
   And, even in gold, they are; for we do find
   Seeds of them, by our fire, and gold in them:
   And can produce the species of each metal
   More perfect thence, than nature doth in earth.   170
   Beside, who doth not see, in daily practice,
   Art can beget bees, hornets, beetles, wasps,
   Out of the carcasses, and dung of creatures;
   Yea, scorpions, of an herb, being rightly placed:
   And these are living creatures, far more perfect,   175
   And excellent, than metals.
MAMMON   Well said, Father!
   Nay, if he take you in hand, sir, with an argument,

145 *crass* dense, thick   157 *means* intermediate stages
164 *hermaphrodeity* combining characteristics of either sex
166 *extensive* i.e. can permeate, or be drawn out, spread out
174 *herb* i.e. basil

He'll bray you in a mortar.
SURLY   Pray you, sir, stay.
Rather, than I'll be brayed, sir, I'll believe,
That alchemy is a pretty kind of game,   180
Somewhat like tricks o' the cards, to cheat a man,
With charming.
SUBTLE   Sir?
SURLY   What else are all your terms,
Whereon no one o' your writers 'grees with other?
Of your elixir, your *lac virginis*,
Your stone, your medicine, and your chrysosperm,   185
Your sal, your sulphur, and your mercury,
Your oil of height, your tree of life, your blood,
Your marcasite, your tutty, your magnesia,
Your toad, your crow, your dragon, and your panther,
Your sun, your moon, your firmament, your adrop,   190
Your lato, azoch, zernich, chibrit, autarit,
And then, your red man, and your white woman,
With all your broths, your menstrues, and materials,
Of piss, and eggshells, women's terms, man's blood,
Hair o' the head, burnt clouts, chalk, merds, and clay,   195
Powder of bones, scalings of iron, glass,
And worlds of other strange ingredients,
Would burst a man to name?
SUBTLE   And all these, named
Intending but one thing: which art our writers
Used to obscure their art.
MAMMON   Sir, so I told him,   200
Because the simple idiot should not learn it,
And make it vulgar.
SUBTLE   Was not all the knowledge
Of the Egyptians writ in mystic symbols?
Speak not the Scriptures, oft, in parables?
Are not the choicest fables of the poets,   205
That were the fountains, and first springs of wisdom,
Wrapped in perplexed allegories?

178 *bray . . . mortar* i.e. crush with pestle, pound. Vide *Proverbs* xxvii,
      22
182 *charming* casting a spell, beguiling
184 *lac virginis* water of mercury   185 *chrysosperm* seed of gold
188 *tutty* impure zinc
190 *adrop* lead
191 *lato* latten, a mixed metal; *azoch* quicksilver; *zernich* trisulphide
      of arsenic; *chibrit* sulphur; *autarit*(*e*) mercury
192 *red man . . . white woman* sulphur and mercury
195 *merds* ordure

MAMMON   I urged that,
  And cleared to him, that Sisyphus was damned
  To roll the ceaseless stone, only, because
  He would have made ours common. Who is this?   210
                    Dol is seen
SUBTLE
  God's precious—What do you mean? Go in, good lady,
  Let me entreat you. Where's this varlet?

                    [*Enter* FACE]

FACE   Sir?
SUBTLE
  You very knave! Do you use me, thus?
FACE   Wherein, sir?
SUBTLE
  Go in, and see, you traitor. Go.   [*Exit* FACE]
MAMMON   Who is it, sir?
SUBTLE
  Nothing, sir. Nothing.
MAMMON   What's the matter? Good, sir!   215
  I have not seen you thus distempered. Who is 't?
SUBTLE
  All arts have still had, sir, their adversaries,

                    FACE *returns*

  But ours the most ignorant. What now?
FACE
  'Twas not my fault, sir, she would speak with you.
SUBTLE
  Would she, sir? Follow me.
MAMMON   Stay, Lungs.
FACE   I dare not, sir.   220
MAMMON
  How! Pray thee stay
FACE   She's mad, sir, and sent hither—
MAMMON
  Stay man, what is she?
FACE   A lord's sister, sir.
  (He'll be mad too.
MAMMON   I warrant thee.) Why sent hither?
FACE
  Sir, to be cured.
SUBTLE [*within*]   Why, rascal!

208 *Sisyphus*. Again, from Delrio, *Disquisit. Mag.* i.66.

FACE   Lo you. Here, sir.
                         He goes out

MAMMON
  'Fore God, a Bradamante, a brave piece.   225
SURLY
  Heart, this is a bawdyhouse! I'll be burnt else.
MAMMON
  O, by this light, no. Do not wrong him. He's
  Too scrupulous, that way. It is his vice.
  No, he's a rare physician, do him right.
  An excellent Paracelsian! And has done   230
  Strange cures with mineral physic. He deals all
  With spirits, he. He will not hear a word
  Of Galen, or his tedious recipes.
                         FACE *again*
  How now, Lungs!
FACE   Softly, sir, speak softly. I meant
  To ha' told your worship all. This must not hear.   235
MAMMON
  No, he will not be gulled; let him alone.
FACE
  You're very right, sir, she is a most rare scholar;
  And is gone mad, with studying Broughton's works.
  If you but name a word, touching the Hebrew,
  She falls into her fit, and will discourse   240
  So learnedly of genealogies,
  As you would run mad, too, to hear her, sir.
MAMMON
  How might one do t'have conference with her, Lungs?
FACE
  O, divers have run mad upon the conference.
  I do not know, sir: I am sent in haste,   245
  To fetch a vial.
SURLY   Be not gulled, Sir Mammon.
MAMMON
  Wherein? Pray ye, be patient.
SURLY   Yes, as you are.
  And trust confederate knaves, and bawds, and whores.

225 *Bradamante* an Amazon (in *Orlando Furioso*)
230 *Paracelsian* Paracelsus (1493–1541) united chemistry with
    medicine
233 i.e. traditional herbs and drugs
235 *This* i.e. Surly
236 *gulled* (ironically intended)
238 *Broughton* a contemporary O.T. theologian
244 i.e. upon merely meeting her

MAMMON
    You are too foul, believe it. Come, here, Eulen.
    One word.
FACE   I dare not, in good faith.
MAMMON   Stay, knave.   250
FACE
    He's extreme angry, that you saw her, sir.
MAMMON
    Drink that. What is she, when she's out of her fit?
FACE
    O, the most affablest creature, sir! So merry!
    So pleasant! She'll mount you up, like quicksilver,
    Over the helm; and circulate, like oil,   255
    A very vegetal: discourse of state,
    Of mathematics, bawdry, anything—
MAMMON
    Is she no way accessible? No means,
    No trick, to give a man a taste of her–wit—
    Or so?
SUBTLE [*within*] Eulen!
FACE   I'll come to you again, sir.   [*Exit* FACE]   260
MAMMON
    Surly, I did not think, one o' your breeding
    Would traduce personages of worth.
SURLY   Sir Epicure,
    Your friend to use: yet, still, loth to be gulled.
    I do not like your philosophical bawds.
    Their stone is lechery enough, to pay for,   265
    Without this bait.
MAMMON   Heart, you abuse yourself.
    I know the lady, and her friends, and means,
    The original of this disaster. Her brother
    Has told me all.
SURLY   And yet, you ne'er saw her
    Till now?
MAMMON   O, yes, but I forgot. I have (believe it)   270
    One of the treacherous'st memories, I do think,
    Of all mankind.
SURLY   What call you her, brother?
MAMMON   My lord—

249 *Eulen* so F (Q has Zephyrus)   252 *Drink that* i.e. a bribe
256 *vegetal* perhaps (Latin) active

259–60 Q has 'Wit? or so?' as the beginning of line 260. In F 'Eulen' is made
    a part of Mammon's speech; Q omits the word altogether. The present
    emendation is Gifford's.

He wi' not have his name known, now I think on't.
SURLY
   A very treacherous memory!
MAMMON   O' my faith—
SURLY
   Tut, if you ha' it not about you, pass it,   275
   Till we meet next.
MAMMON   Nay, by this hand, 'tis true.
   He's one I honour, and my noble friend,
   And I respect his house.
SURLY   Heart! Can it be,
   That a grave sir, a rich, that has no need,
   A wise sir, too, at other times, should thus   280
   With his own oaths, and arguments, make hard means
   To gull himself? And, this be your elixir,
   Your *lapis mineralis*, and your lunary,
   Give me your honest trick, yet, at primero,
   Or gleek; and take your *lutum sapientis*,   285
   Your *menstruum simplex:* I'll have gold, before you,
   And, with less danger of the quicksilver;
   Or the hot sulphur.

[*Enter* FACE]

FACE   Here's one from Captain Face, sir,
To SURLY
   Desires you meet him i' the Temple Church,
   Some half hour hence, and upon earnest business.   290
   Sir, if you please to quit us, now; and come,
He whispers MAMMON
   Again, within two hours: you shall have,
   My master busy examining o' the works;
   And I will steal you in, unto the party,
   That you may see her converse. [*To* SURLY]
                       Sir, shall I say,   295
   You'll meet the Captain's worship?
SURLY   Sir, I will.
   But, by attorney, and to a second purpose.

281 *hard* harsh
283 *lunary* the fern, moonwort, whose 'liquor' was connected with
    making silver
285 *gleek* a card game; *lutum* philosopher's lute, or clay
286 *menstruum* plain solvent
287 (with side-glance at venereal diseases and scabies)
289 *Temple Church* the Round, a usual meeting-place
295 *converse* euphemistically, for sexual attractions
297 *attorney* in another's person

Now, I am sure, it is a bawdy house;
I'll swear it, were the Marshal here, to thank me:
The naming this Commander, doth confirm it.   300
Don Face! Why, he's the most authentic dealer
I' these commodities! The Superintendent
To all the quainter traffickers, in town.
He is their Visitor, and does appoint
Who lies with whom; and at what hour; what price;   305
Which gown; and in what smock; what fall; what tire.
Him, will I prove, by a third person, to find
The subleties of this dark labyrinth:
Which, if I do discover, dear Sir Mammon,
You'll give your poor friend leave, though no philosopher, 310
To laugh: for you that are, 'tis thought, shall weep.

FACE
Sir. He does pray, you'll not forget.

SURLY   I will not, sir.
Sir Epicure, I shall leave you?   [*Exit* SURLY]

MAMMON   I follow you, straight.

FACE
But do so, good sir, to avoid suspicion.
This gentleman has a parlous head.

MAMMON   But wilt thou, Eulen,   315
Be constant to thy promise?

FACE   As my life, sir.

MAMMON
And wilt thou insinuate what I am? And praise me?
And say I am a noble fellow?

FACE   O, what else, sir?
And, that you'll make her royal, with the stone,
An empress; and yourself King of Bantam.   320

MAMMON
Wilt thou do this?

FACE   Will I, sir?

MAMMON   Lungs, my Lungs!
I love thee.

FACE   Send your stuff, sir, that my master
May busy himself, about projection.

299 *Marshal* provost
300 *Commander* another euphemism; so *Superintendent, quainter, Visitor*
306 *fall* loose collar, as against stiff ruff; *tire* apron (primarily; but see *O.E.D.* for euphemistic suggestions)
315 *parlous* (perilous) here, shrewd, penetrating
320 *Bantam* Javanese city, newly opened to trade: associated with dreams of wealth

MAMMON
  Th'hast witched me, rogue: take, go.
FACE   Your jack, and all, sir.
MAMMON
  Thou art a villain–I will send my jack;   325
  And the weights too. Slave, I could bite thine ear.
  Away, thou dost not care for me.
FACE   Not I, sir?
MAMMON
  Come, I was born to make thee, my good weasel;
  Set thee on a bench: and, ha' thee twirl a chain
  With the best lord's vermin, of 'em all.
FACE   Away, sir.   330
MAMMON
  A count, nay, a count-palatine—
FACE   Good sir, go.
MAMMON
  Shall not advance thee, better: no, nor faster.
                                        [*Exit* MAMMON]

Act II, Scene iv

[*Enter*] SUBTLE, DOL

SUBTLE
  Has he bit? Has he bit?
FACE   And swallowed too, my Subtle.
  I ha' given him line, and now he plays, i' faith.
SUBTLE
  And shall we twitch him?
FACE   Thorough both the gills.
  A wench is a rare bait, with which a man
  No sooner's taken, but he straight firks mad.   5
SUBTLE
  Dol, my Lord Wha'ts'hum's sister, you must now
  Bear yourself *statelich*.
DOL   O, let me alone.
  I'll not forget my race, I warrant you.
  I'll keep my distance, laugh, and talk aloud;
  Have all the tricks of a proud scurvy lady,   10
  And be as rude's her woman.

324 *jack* mechanism to regulate heat supply
326 *bite thine ear* i.e. amorously
330 *vermin* punning on ermine
  5 *firks mad* is stirred to raging madness
  7 *statelich* stately (German, or Dutch: printed as German in F)

FACE   Well said, Sanguine.
SUBTLE
  But will he send his andirons?
FACE   His jack too;
  And's iron shoeing horn: I ha' spoke to him. Well,
  I must not lose my wary gamester, yonder.
SUBTLE
  O Monsieur Caution, that will not be gulled?   15
FACE
  Ay, if I can strike a fine hook into him, now,
  The Temple Church, there I have cast mine angle.
  Well, pray for me. I'll about it.
SUBTLE   What, more gudgeons!
                      One knocks
  Dol, scout, scout; stay Face, you must go to the door:
  Pray God, it be my Anabaptist. Who is't, Dol?   20
DOL
  I know him not. He looks like a gold-end-man.
SUBTLE
  Gods so! 'Tis he, he said he would send. What call you him?
  The sanctified Elder, that should deal
  For Mammon's jack, and andirons! Let him in.
  Stay, help me off, first, with my gown. Away   25
  Madam, to your withdrawing chamber. Now,   [*Exit* DOL]
  In a new tune, new gesture, but old language.
  This fellow is sent, from one negotiates with me
  About the stone, too; for the holy Brethren
  Of Amsterdam, the exiled Saints: that hope   30
  To raise their discipline, by it. I must use him
  In some strange fashion, now, to make him admire me.

11 *Sanguine* i.e. (here) amorous of disposition
18 *gudgeons* (will swallow anything)
21 *gold-end-man* like modern collector of 'old gold and silver,
    brassware, etc.'
30 *exiled Saints* puritans who had fled abroad (to Geneva, Amster-
    dam and elsewhere)

20 *Anabaptist.* This sect is first known in Germany in 1521, and began to
    appear in England around 1534. It attempted to set up a theocracy, and
    advocated adult baptism and community of goods.

Act II, Scene v

[*Enter*] ANANIAS

SUBTLE

Where is my drudge?

FACE   Sir.

SUBTLE   Take away the recipient,

And rectify your menstrue, from the phlegma.

Then pour it, o' the Sol, in the cucurbite,

And let 'em macerate, together.

FACE   Yes, sir.

And save the ground?

SUBTLE   No. *Terra damnata*   5

Must not have entrance, in the work. Who are you?

ANANIAS

A faithful Brother, if it please you.

SUBTLE   What's that?

A Lullianist? A Ripley? *Filius artis*?

Can you sublime, and dulcify? Calcine?

Know you the *sapor pontic*? *Sapor styptic*?   10

Or, what is the homogene, or heterogene?

ANANIAS

I understand no heathen language, truly.

SUBTLE

Heathen, you Knipperdoling? Is *Ars sacra*,

Or *chrysopoeia*, or *spagyrica*,

1 *recipient* receptacle
2 *phlegma* watery product of distillation
4 *macerate* soften by soaking
5 *ground . . . Terra* i.e. the sediment
9 *sublime* process for solids similar to distillation for liquids;
  dulcify neutralize acidity; eliminate salts; *Calcine* reduce to
  powder by intense heat
10 *sapor* i.e. trial by taste; *pontic* sour; *styptic* astringent
14 *chrysopoeia* making of gold; *spagyrica* alchemical wisdom

8 *A Lullianist? A Ripley?* Two celebrated alchemists. Subtle deliberately
misunderstands Ananias's 'A faithful Brother' as meaning an alchemist.
Raymond Lully (1235–1315) was a Spanish courtier, missionary, al-
chemist, and inventor of a machine for logic, by which one could try
mechanically all possible aspects of a given proposition. Sir George
Ripley, canon of Bridlington, died *circa* 1490. His chief works are *The
Compound of Alchemie* (written 1471, published 1591), and *Medulla
Alchemiae*, 1476.

13 *Knipperdoling*. Bernt Knipperdollinck, a draper, was an Anabaptist
leader in the Munster Rising (1534), when 'the Kingdom of God' was
established there under John of Leyden. The main features of this
kingdom were debauchery and despotism.

Of the pamphysic, or panarchic knowledge,   15
A heathen language?

ANANIAS   Heathen Greek, I take it.

SUBTLE

How? Heathen Greek?

ANANIAS   All's heathen, but the Hebrew.

SUBTLE

Sirrah, my varlet, stand you forth, and speak to him
Like a philosopher: answer, i' the language.
Name the vexations, and the martyrizations   20
Of metals, in the work.

FACE   Sir, Putrefaction,
Solution, Ablution, Sublimation,
Cohobation, Calcination, Ceration, and
Fixation.

SUBTLE   This is heathen Greek, to you, now?
And when comes Vivification?

FACE   After Mortification.   25

SUBTLE

What's Cohobation?

FACE   'Tis the pouring on
Your *Aqua Regis*, and then drawing him off,
To the trine circle of the seven spheres.

SUBTLE

What's the proper passion of metals?

FACE   Malleation.

SUBTLE

What's your *ultimum supplicium auri*?

FACE   *Antimonium.*   30

SUBTLE

This 's heathen Greek, to you? And, what's your mercury?

FACE

A very fugitive, he will be gone, sir.

15 *pamphysic* relating to all nature; *panarchic* sovereign, entire
19 *philosopher* i.e. alchemist
20 i.e. the chemical processes undergone
21 *Putrefaction* decomposition caused by chemical action
22 *Ablution* washing away impure accretions
23 *Cohobation* redistillation; *Ceration* fixation of mercury
24 *Fixation* reduction to permanent form by combination
25 *Vivification* restoring to natural state; *Mortification* alteration of
    form of metals; destruction or neutralization of active qualities
    of chemicals
27 *Aqua Regis* chemical solvent for gold
28 *trine circle* triple; also ('trinity') planets in benign conjunction
29 *passion* natural susceptibility; *Malleation* malleability
30 Gold loses malleability when alloyed with antimony (HS)

SUBTLE
How know you him?
FACE   By his viscosity,
His oleosity, and his suscitability.
SUBTLE
How do you sublime him?
FACE   With the calce of eggshells,   35
White marble, talc.
SUBTLE   Your *magisterium*, now?
What's that?
FACE   Shifting, sir, your elements,
Dry into cold, cold into moist, moist into
Hot, hot into dry.
SUBTLE   This 's heathen Greek to you, still?
Your *lapis philosophicus*?
FACE   'Tis a stone, and not   40
A stone; a spirit, a soul, and a body:
Which, if you do dissolve, it is dissolved,
If you coagulate, it is coagulated,
If you make it to fly, it flieth.
SUBTLE   Enough.   [*Exit* FACE]
This 's heathen Greek, to you? What are you, sir?   45
ANANIAS
Please you, a servant of the exiled Brethren,
That deal with widows; and with orphans' goods;
And make a just account, unto the Saints:
A Deacon.
SUBTLE   O, you are sent from master Wholesome,
Your teacher?
ANANIAS   From Tribulation Wholesome,   50
Our very zealous Pastor.
SUBTLE   Good. I have
Some orphans' goods to come here.
ANANIAS   Of what kind, sir?
SUBTLE
Pewter, and brass, andirons, and kitchen ware,
Metals, that we must use our medicine on:
Wherein the Brethren may have a penn'orth,   55
For ready money.
ANANIAS   Were the orphans' parents

---

34 *oleosity* oiliness; *suscitability* excitability
35 *calce* calx, powder
36 *magisterium* token of alchemical mastery
37 *elements* i.e. the four elements
48 *Saints* i.e. the Faithful of the sect. N.T. usage

Sincere professors?

SUBTLE   Why do you ask?

ANANIAS   Because
We then are to deal justly, and give (in truth)
Their utmost value.

SUBTLE   'Slid, you'd cozen, else,
And, if their parents were not of the faithful?   60
I will not trust you, now I think on 't,
Till I ha' talked with your Pastor. Ha' you brought money
To buy more coals?

ANANIAS   No, surely.

SUBTLE   No? How so?

ANANIAS
The Brethren bid me say unto you, sir.
Surely, they will not venture any more,   65
Till they may see projection.

SUBTLE   How!

ANANIAS   You've had,
For the instruments, as bricks, and loam, and glasses,
Already thirty pound; and, for materials,
They say, some ninety more: and, they have heard, since,
That one, at Heidelberg, made it, of an egg,   70
And a small paper of pin-dust.

SUBTLE   What's your name?

ANANIAS
My name is Ananias.

SUBTLE   Out, the varlet
That cozened the Apostles! Hence, away,
Flee mischief; had your holy Consistory
No name to send me, of another sound;   75
Than wicked Ananias? Send your Elders,
Hither, to make atonement for you, quickly.
And gi' me satisfaction; or out goes
The fire: and down th' alembics, and the furnace,
Piger Henricus, or what not. Thou wretch,   80
Both Sericon, and Bufo, shall be lost,
Tell 'em. All hope of rooting out the Bishops,

57 *professors* i.e. of the Faith
67 *instruments* necessary materials, means
70 *one, at Heidelberg* not traced. Mere rumour?
71 *pin-dust* fine metallic dust (used in making pins)
73 *That cozened* See *Acts* v (for Subtle's view) and ix (for Ananias's, no doubt)
80 *Piger Henricus* (lazy Henry) a composite furnace
81 *Sericon* ingredient in Alchemists' gold: red tincture; *Bufo* (toad) black tincture

Or th' Antichristian Hierarchy shall perish,
If they stay threescore minutes. The Aqueity,
Terreity, and Sulphureity   85
Shall run together again, and all be annulled
Thou wicked Ananias. This will fetch 'em,

                                    [*Exit* ANANIAS]

And make 'em haste towards their gulling more.
A man must deal like a rough nurse, and fright
Those, that are froward, to an appetite.   90

Act II, Scene vi

[*Enter*] DRUGGER, FACE

FACE

He's busy with his spirits, but we'll upon him.

SUBTLE

How now! What mates? What Bayards ha' we here?

FACE

I told you, he would be furious. Sir, here's Nab,
Has brought you another piece of gold, to look on:
(We must appease him. Give it me) and prays you,   5
You would devise (what is it Nab?)

DRUGGER   A sign, sir.

FACE

Ay, a good lucky one, a thriving sign, Doctor.

SUBTLE

I was devising now.

FACE   ('Slight, do not say so,
He will repent he ga' you any more.)
What say you to his constellation, Doctor?   10
The Balance?

SUBTLE   No, that way is stale, and common.
A townsman, born in Taurus, gives the bull;
Or the bull's head: in Aries, the ram.
A poor device. No, I will have his name

---

84 *Aqueity* clarified mercury
 2 *Bayards* ('Bold as blind Bayards') from the legendary horse of
   Charlemagne
11 *The Balance* see I.iii, 56 ff.

---

83 *Antichristian Hierarchy*. Puritan opposition to episcopacy, which came
   to a climax in the Civil War, was present from much earlier times.
   Herford and Simpson quote from a work of John Udall, dated 1588.
   The use which Ananias and Tribulation intended for the stone is
   detailed in the opening scenes of Act III.

Formed in some mystic character; whose radii,   15
Striking the senses of the passers-by,
Shall, by a virtual influence, breed affections,
That may result upon the party owns it:
As thus—

FACE   Nab!

SUBTLE   He first shall have a bell, that's Abel;
And, by it, standing one, whose name is Dee,   20
In a rug gown; there's D and Rug, that's Drug:
And, right anenst him, a dog snarling Er;
There's Drugger, Abel Drugger. That's his sign.
And here's now mystery, and hieroglyphic!

FACE

Abel, thou art made.

DRUGGER   Sir, I do thank his worship.   25

FACE

Six o' thy legs more, will not do it, Nab.
He has brought you a pipe of tobacco, Doctor.

DRUGGER   Yes, sir:
I have another thing, I would impart—

FACE

Out with it, Nab.

DRUGGER   Sir, there is lodged, hard by me
A rich young widow—

FACE   Good! A *bona roba*?   30

DRUGGER

But nineteen, at the most.

FACE   Very good, Abel.

DRUGGER

Marry, she's not in fashion, yet; she wears
A hood: but 't stands a cop.

FACE   No matter, Abel.

DRUGGER

And, I do, now and then give her a fucus—

FACE

What! Dost thou deal, Nab?

SUBTLE   I did tell you, Captain.   35

17 *virtual* powerful, of virtue; *affections* inclinations, appetites
22 *anenst* opposite   26 *legs* bows
30 *bona roba* (buona roba) lit. finely dressed girl; loosely, comely
girl, 'fine piece'
33 *hood* (as opposed to fashionable hats); *a cop* high on the head
34 *fucus* cosmetic   35 *deal* i.e. in cosmetics, philtres, etc.

20 *Dee.* John Dee (1527–1608) was an astrologer and mathematician, part
scholar and part quack, who was employed by Queen Elizabeth.

DRUGGER
　　And physic too sometime, sir: for which she trusts me
　　With all her mind. She's come up here, of purpose
　　To learn the fashion.
FACE　　　　　　　　Good (his match too!) on, Nab.
DRUGGER
　　And she does strangely long to know her fortune.
FACE
　　God's lid, Nab, send her to the Doctor, hither.　　　　40
DRUGGER
　　Yes, I have spoke to her of his worship, already:
　　But she's afraid, it will be blown abroad
　　And hurt her marriage.
FACE　　　　　　　Hurt it? 'Tis the way
　　To heal it, if 'twere hurt; to make it more
　　Followed, and sought: Nab, thou shalt tell her this.　　45
　　She'll be more known, more talked of, and your widows
　　Are ne'er of any price till they be famous;
　　Their honour is their multitude of suitors:
　　Send her, it may be thy good fortune. What?
　　Thou dost not know.
DRUGGER　　　　No, sir, she'll never marry　　　50
　　Under a knight. Her brother has made a vow.
FACE
　　What, and dost thou despair, my little Nab,
　　Knowing, what the Doctor has set down for thee,
　　And, seeing so many, o' the city, dubbed?
　　One glass o' thy water, with a Madam, I know,　　　55
　　Will have it done, Nab. What's her brother? A knight?
DRUGGER
　　No, sir, a gentleman, newly warm in his land, sir,
　　Scarce cold in his one and twenty; that does govern
　　His sister, here: and is a man himself
　　Of some three thousand a year, and is come up　　　60
　　To learn to quarrel, and to live by his wits,
　　And will go down again, and die i' the country.
FACE
　　How! To quarrel?
DRUGGER　　　　Yes, sir, to carry quarrels,
　　As gallants do, and manage 'em, by line.
FACE
　　'Slid, Nab! The Doctor is the only man　　　65

54 *dubbed* knighted
55 *thy water* probably a love philtre
64 *by line* conforming accurately to etiquette

In Christendom for him. He has made a table,
With mathematical demonstrations,
Touching the art of quarrels. He will give him
An instrument to quarrel by. Go, bring 'em, both:
Him, and his sister. And, for thee, with her   70
The Doctor haply may persuade. Go to.
Shalt give his worship, a new damask suit
Upon the premises.

SUBTLE   O, good Captain.

FACE   He shall,
He is the honestest fellow, Doctor. Stay not,
No offers, bring the damask, and the parties.   75

DRUGGER
I'll try my power, sir.

FACE   And thy will too, Nab.

SUBTLE
'Tis good tobacco this! What is't an ounce?

FACE
He'll send you a pound, Doctor.

SUBTLE   O, no.

FACE   He will do't.
It is the goodest soul. Abel, about it.
(Thou shalt know more anon. Away, be gone.)   80
                                        [*Exit* DRUGGER]
A miserable rogue, and lives with cheese,
And has the worms. That was the cause indeed
Why he came now. He dealt with me, in private,
To get a medicine for 'em.

SUBTLE   And shall, sir. This works.

FACE
A wife, a wife, for one on's, my dear Subtle: 85
We'll e'en draw lots, and he, that fails, shall have
The more in goods, the other has in tail.

SUBTLE
Rather the less. For she may be so light
She may want grains.

FACE   Ay, or be such a burden,
A man would scarce endure her, for the whole.   90

SUBTLE
Faith, best let's see her first, and then determine.

---

71 *haply* ed. (F, Q have *happ'ly*)
73 *premises* here, promising grounds for hope
88 *light* wanton (punningly). Bawdy insinuations **continue in lines**
    following

FACE

Content. But Dol must ha' no breath on't.

SUBTLE   Mum.

Away, you to your Surly yonder, catch him.

FACE

Pray God, I ha' not stayed too long.

SUBTLE   I fear it.

[*Exeunt*]

Act III, Scene i

[*Enter*] TRIBULATION, ANANIAS

TRIBULATION

These chastisements are common to the Saints,
And such rebukes we of the Separation
Must bear, with willing shoulders, as the trials
Sent forth, to tempt our frailties.

ANANIAS   In pure zeal,
I do not like the man: he is a heathen.   5
And speaks the language of Canaan, truly.

TRIBULATION

I think him a profane person, indeed.

ANANIAS   He bears
The visible mark of the Beast, in his forehead.
And for his stone, it is a work of darkness,
And, with philosophy, blinds the eyes of man.   10

TRIBULATION

Good Brother, we must bend unto all means,
That may give furtherance, to the holy cause.

ANANIAS

Which his cannot: the sanctified cause
Should have a sanctified course.

TRIBULATION   Not always necessary.
The children of perdition are ofttimes,   15
Made instruments even of the greatest works.
Beside, we should give somewhat to man's nature,
The place he lives in, still about the fire,
And fume of metals, that intoxicate
The brain of man, and make him prone to passion.   20

4 *pure zeal* i.e. without personal malice
6 *of Canaan* see *Isaiah* xix
8 *mark of the Beast* see *Revelation* xvi and xix; allusion to Subtle's
    velvet cap
10 extreme Puritans damned all learning
11 *bend* shape ourselves, concede
17 *give* make allowances

Where have you greater atheists, than your cooks?
Or more profane, or choleric than your glassmen?
More antichristian, than your bellfounders?
What makes the Devil so devilish, I would ask you,
Satan, our common enemy, but his being   25
Perpetually about the fire, and boiling
Brimstone, and arsenic? We must give, I say,
Unto the motives, and the stirrers up
Of humours in the blood. It may be so.
When as the work is done, the stone is made,   30
This heat of his may turn into a zeal,
And stand up for the beauteous discipline,
Against the menstruous cloth, and rag of Rome.
We must await his calling, and the coming
Of the good spirit. You did fault, t' upbraid him   35
With the Brethren's blessing of Heidelberg, weighing
What need we have, to hasten on the work,
For the restoring of the silenced Saints,
Which ne'er will be, but by the philosopher's stone.
And, so a learned Elder, one of Scotland,   40
Assured me; *aurum potabile* being
The only medicine, for the civil magistrate,
T' incline him to a feeling of the cause:
And must be daily used, in the disease.

ANANIAS
    I have not edified more, truly, by man;   45
Not, since the beautiful light, first, shone on me:
And I am sad, my zeal hath so offended.

TRIBULATION
    Let us call on him, then.

ANANIAS   The motion's good,
    And of the spirit; I will knock first: peace be within.

---

21 *atheists* (loosely used) profane or godless men
28 *motives* forces (as here the fire) that stimulate, generate, move one
36 see II.v, 70
41 *aurum potabile* medicinal gold; a term for the elixir common in
    alchemy. Side glance at bribery
45 *edified* taken more wholesome spiritual fare
48 *motion* impulse

---

38 *silenced Saints.* After the Hampton Court conference (1604) the clergy
    in convocation passed canons regulating public worship and excommuni-
    cating all who denied the supremacy of the King, refused the Prayer
    Book or the Thirty Nine Articles, or separated from the church. Esti-
    mates of those affected vary from fifty to three hundred. They, and their
    followers, were the 'silenced ministers'. Cf. *Epicoene*, II.ii, 80.

Act III, Scene ii

[*Enter*] SUBTLE, TRIBULATION, ANANIAS

SUBTLE
O, are you come? 'Twas time. Your threescore minutes
Were at the last thread, you see; and down had gone
Furnus acediae, turris circulatorius:
Lembic, bolt's head, retort, and pelican
Had all been cinders. Wicked Ananias!   5
Art thou returned? Nay then, it goes down, yet.
TRIBULATION
Sir, be appeased, he is come to humble
Himself in spirit, and to ask your patience,
If too much zeal hath carried him, aside,
From the due path.
SUBTLE   Why, this doth qualify!   10
TRIBULATION
The Brethren had no purpose, verily,
To give you the least grievance: but are ready
To lend their willing hands, to any project
The spirit, and you direct.
SUBTLE   This qualifies more!
TRIBULATION
And, for the orphans' goods, let them be valued,   15
Or what is needful, else, to the holy work,
It shall be numbered: here, by me, the Saints
Throw down their purse before you.
SUBTLE   This qualifies, most!
Why, thus it should be, now you understand.
Have I discoursed so unto you, of our stone?   20
And, of the good that it shall bring your cause?
Showed you, (beside the main of hiring forces
Abroad, drawing the Hollanders, your friends,
From th' Indies, to serve you, with all their fleet)
That even the medicinal use shall make you a faction,   25
And party in the realm? As, put the case,
That some great man in state, he have the gout,
Why, you but send three drops of your elixir,

3 *Furnus acediae* a compound furnace. See II.v, 80 ('lazy Henry');
   turris circulatorius circulatory, special retort for distillation
4 *Lembic* alembic
17 *numbered* added, included
25 *make you a faction* create partisan supporters

You help him straight: there you have made a friend.
Another has the palsy, or the dropsy,   30
He takes of your incombustible stuff,
He's young again: there you have made a friend.
A lady, that is past the feat of body,
Though not of mind, and hath her face decayed
Beyond all cure of paintings, you restore   35
With the oil of talc; there you have made a friend:
And all her friends. A lord, that is a leper,
A knight, that has the bone-ache, or a squire
That hath both these, you make 'em smooth, and sound,
With a bare fricace of your medicine: still,   40
You increase your friends.

TRIBULATION   Ay, 'tis very pregnant.

SUBTLE
And, then, the turning of this lawyer's pewter
To plate, at Christmas—

ANANIAS   Christ-tide, I pray you.

SUBTLE
Yet, Ananias?

ANANIAS   I have done.

SUBTLE   Or changing
His parcel gilt, to massy gold. You cannot   45
But raise you friends. With all, to be of power
To pay an army, in the field, to buy
The King of France, out of his realms; or Spain,
Out of his Indies: what can you not do,
Against lords spiritual, or temporal,   50
That shall oppone you?

TRIBULATION   Verily, 'tis true.
We may be temporal lords, ourselves, I take it.

SUBTLE
You may be anything, and leave off to make
Long-winded exercises: or suck up,

31 *incombustible stuff* incombustible oil was among the forms of the
   final alchemical 'miracle'
33 *feat* featness, fitness, elegance
36 *oil of talc* the philosopher's oil, again; 'the white elixir'
40 *fricace* light friction
45 *parcel gilt* partly gilded silverware
51 *oppone* oppose
54 *exercises* extempore effusions of the 'moved' spirit, perhaps
   sermons also

---

43 *Christ-tide.* The 'Popish' word *mass* was scrupulously avoided by the
   Puritans. Similarly, they refused to use saints' names for streets; St.
   Anne's Street became Anne Street.

Your ha, and hum, in a tune. I not deny,   55
But such as are not graced, in a state,
May, for their ends, be adverse in religion,
And get a tune, to call the flock together:
For (to say sooth) a tune does much, with women,
And other phlegmatic people, it is your bell.   60

ANANIAS

Bells are profane: a tune may be religious.

SUBTLE

No warning with you? Then, farewell my patience.
'Slight, it shall down: I will not be thus tortured.

TRIBULATION

I pray you, sir.

SUBTLE   All shall perish. I have spoke it.

TRIBULATION

Let me find grace, sir, in your eyes; the man   65
He stands corrected: neither did his zeal
(But as yourself) allow a tune, somewhere.
Which, now, being toward the stone, we shall not need.

SUBTLE

No, nor your holy vizard, to win widows
To give you legacies; or make zealous wives   70
To rob their husbands, for the common cause:
Nor take the start of bonds, broke but one day,
And say, they were forfeited, by providence.
Nor shall you need, o'er night, to eat huge meals,
To celebrate your next day's fast the better: 75
The whilst the Brethren, and the Sisters, humbled,
Abate the stiffness of the flesh. Nor cast
Before your hungry hearers, scrupulous bones,
As whether a Christian may hawk, or hunt;
Or whether, matrons, of the holy assembly,   80

55 alludes to preaching mannerisms; *not deny* do not deny
56 *graced* advantaged, as by established religious forms
63 *shall down* alludes to earlier threat of demolition
67 (*But as* . . .) except in so far as
69 *vizard* feigned facial expression
72 *take the start* gain the advantage, by acting smartly
77 *Abate the stiffness* beat down the rigid, inflexible (disposition, unchastened desire, will)
78 *scrupulous bones* contentious issues depending on fine scruples, minute distinctions

69–82 *No, nor your holy vizard* &c. A catalogue of the common charges against Puritans. Compare Dame Purecraft's speech on the same subject in *Bartholomew Fair*, V.ii.

May lay their hair out, or wear doublets:
Or have that idol Starch, about their linen.
ANANIAS
    It is, indeed, an idol.
TRIBULATION   Mind him not, sir.
    I do command thee, spirit (of zeal, but trouble)
    To peace within him. Pray you, sir, go on.   85
SUBTLE
    Nor shall you need to libel 'gainst the prelates,
    And shorten so your ears, against the hearing
    Of the next wire-drawn grace. Nor, of necessity,
    Rail against plays, to please the alderman,
    Whose daily custard you devour. Nor lie   90
    With zealous rage, till you are hoarse. Not one
    Of these so singular arts. Nor call yourselves,
    By names of Tribulation, Persecution,
    Restraint, Long-Patience, and such like, affected
    By the whole family, or wood of you,   95
    Only for glory, and to catch the ear
    Of the Disciple.
TRIBULATION   Truly, sir, they are
    Ways, that the godly Brethren have invented,
    For propagation of the glorious cause,
    As very notable means, and whereby, also,   100
    Themselves grow soon, and profitably famous.
SUBTLE
    O, but the stone, all's idle to it! Nothing!
    The art of Angels, nature's miracle,
    The divine secret, that doth fly in clouds,
    From east to west: and whose tradition   105
    Is not from men, but spirits.
ANANIAS   I hate traditions:
    I do not trust 'em—
TRIBULATION   Peace.
ANANIAS   They are popish, all.
    I will not peace. I will not—

87 *shorten so* alludes to punishment of cutting off ears
88 *wire-drawn grace* i.e. long-drawn-out, and thin, tenuous: as in the
    extraction of wire: a frequent metaphoric jibe at the time
89 *alderman* used to connote the plural; city magistrates
95 *wood* crowd
100 *notable* likely to catch attention

106 *I hate traditions.* Puritans held the Bible to be the only rule of faith
    and practice. The Jews and the Roman Church believed religious tra-
    ditions to be of some value. Hence they were Popish and anathema.

TRIBULATION   Ananias.

ANANIAS
  Please the profane, to grieve the godly: I may not.
SUBTLE
  Well, Ananias, thou shalt overcome.   110
TRIBULATION
  It is an ignorant zeal, that haunts him, sir.
  But truly, else, a very faithful Brother,
  A botcher: and a man, by revelation,
  That hath a competent knowledge of the truth
SUBTLE
  Has he a competent sum, there, i' the bag,   115
  To buy the goods, within? I am made guardian,
  And must, for charity, and conscience' sake,
  Now, see the most be made, for my poor orphan:
  Though I desire the Brethren, too, good gainers.
  There, they are, within. When you have viewed, and
                              bought 'em,   120
  And ta'en the inventory of what they are,
  They are ready for projection; there's no more
  To do: cast on the medicine, so much silver
  As there is tin there, so much gold as brass,
  I'll gi' it you in, by weight.
TRIBULATION   But how long time,   125
  Sir, must the Saints expect, yet?
SUBTLE   Let me see,
  How's the moon, now? Eight, nine, ten days hence
  He will be silver potate; then, three days,
  Before he citronize: some fifteen days,
  The *magisterium* will be perfected.   130
ANANIAS
  About the second day, of the third week,
  In the ninth month?
SUBTLE   Yes, my good Ananias.
TRIBULATION
  What will the orphan's goods arise to, think you?
SUBTLE
  Some hundred marks; as much as filled three cars,
  Unladed now: you'll make six millions of 'em.   135
  But I must ha' more coals laid in.

110 N.T. phrase used punningly: 'you will be too much for us'
113 *botcher* repairing tailor
126 *expect* await the consummation
128 *silver potate* liquefied silver (HS)
129 *citronize* achieve the colour denoting alchemical consummation

TRIBULATION   How!
SUBTLE   Another load,
  And then we ha' finished. We must now increase
  Our fire to *ignis ardens*, we are past
  Fimus equinus, balnei, cineris,
  And all those lenter heats. If the holy purse   140
  Should, with this draught, fall low, and that the Saints
  Do need a present sum, I have a trick
  To melt the pewter, you shall buy now, instantly,
  And, with a tincture, make you as good Dutch dollars,
  As any are in Holland.
TRIBULATION   Can you so?   145
SUBTLE
  Ay, and shall bide the third examination.
ANANIAS
  It will be joyful tidings to the Brethren.
SUBTLE
  But you must carry it, secret.
TRIBULATION   Ay, but stay,
  This act of coining, is it lawful?
ANANIAS   Lawful?
  We know no magistrate. Or, if we did,   150
  This 's foreign coin.
SUBTLE   It is no coining, sir.
  It is but casting.
TRIBULATION   Ha? You distinguish well.
  Casting of money may be lawful.
ANANIAS   'Tis, sir.
TRIBULATION
  Truly, I take it so.

138 *ignis ardens* the hottest fire
139 *Fimus equinus* moist heat (from 'horse dung'); *balnei* warmth (of
    water) just below boiling; *cineris* denotes the next stage of heat
    (see II.iii, 41, 85)
140 *lenter* slower
142 *a trick* so F2 (F1, Q, have *I have trick*)
146 i.e. survive legal or police investigation
150 *know* acknowledge

---

150 *We know no magistrate.* Some Puritans rejected all human forms of
    government as carnal ordinances, and set up the scripture as the only
    civil code. The Confession of Faith of the English Baptists at Amsterdam
    in 1611 expressly stated that 'the magistrate is not to meddle in religion
    or matters of conscience'. A surprising variety of things could become
    'matters of conscience'.
151 *foreign coin.* Counterfeiting of *foreign* coin first became high treason in
    the reign of Queen Mary. 'Coining' was already a capital offence, and as
    late as 1786 a woman was executed for coining silver.

SUBTLE   There is no scruple,
  Sir, to be made of it; believe Ananias: 155
  This case of conscience he is studied in.
TRIBULATION
  I'll make a question of it, to the Brethren.
ANANIAS
  The Brethren shall approve it lawful, doubt not.
  Where shall't be done?
SUBTLE   For that we'll talk, anon.
                 Knock without
  There's some to speak with me. Go in, I pray you,   160
  And view the parcels. That's the inventory.
            [*Exeunt* ANANIAS, TRIBULATION]
  I'll come to you straight. Who is it? Face! Appear.

Act III, Scene iii

[*Enter*] FACE

SUBTLE
  How now? Good prize?
FACE   Good pox! Yond' costive cheater
  Never came on.
SUBTLE   How then?
FACE   I ha' walked the round,
  Till now, and no such thing.
SUBTLE   And ha' you quit him?
FACE
  Quit him? And hell would quit him too, he were happy.
  'Slight would you have me stalk like a mill-jade,   5
  All day, for one, that will not yield us grains?
  I know him of old.
SUBTLE   O, but to ha' gulled him,
  Had been a mastery.
FACE   Let him go, black boy,
  And turn thee, that some fresh news may possess thee.
  A noble count, a don of Spain (my dear   10

2 *walked the round* kept a look out (with side glance at the Temple
  Church 'round')
4 i.e. I certainly have
5 *mill-jade* tired old horse moving round and round
6 food, weight (sustaining the metaphor)

8 *black boy.* Horace, *Satires*, I.iv. 85, 'hic niger est, hunc tu, Romane,
caveto'. Cf. *Every Man Out of his Humour*, I.ii, 210.

Delicious compeer, and my party-bawd)
Who is come hither, private, for his conscience,
And brought munition with him, six great slops,
Bigger than three Dutch hoys, beside round trunks,
Furnished with pistolets, and pieces of eight,   15
Will straight be here, my rogue, to have thy bath
(That is the colour,) and to make his battery
Upon our Dol, our castle, our Cinque-Port,
Our Dover pier, our what thou wilt. Where is she?
She must prepare perfumes, delicate linen,   20
The bath in chief, a banquet, and her wit,
For she must milk his epididymis.
Where is the doxy?

SUBTLE   I'll send her to thee:
And but despatch my brace of little John Leydens,
And come again myself.

FACE   Are they within then?   25

SUBTLE
Numbering the sum.

FACE   How much?

SUBTLE   A hundred marks, boy.
                                              [*Exit* SUBTLE]

FACE
Why, this 's a lucky day! Ten pounds of Mammon!
Three o' my clerk! A portague o' my grocer!
This o' the Brethren! Beside reversions,
And states, to come i' the widow, and my count!   30
                    [*Enter* DOL]
My share, today, will not be bought for forty—

DOL   What?

FACE
Pounds, dainty Dorothy, art thou so near?

---

11 *compeer* comrade (properly, godfather); *party-bawd* partner in
   bawdry
13 *slops* fashionable nether garment
14 *hoys* small vessels, usually sloop-rigged (see previous line); *round
   trunks* large breeches, worn padded
15 *pistolets* Spanish gold pieces, worth nearly £1
17 *colour* official pretext
18 *Cinque-Port* five privileged sea ports on the south coast
19 the metaphor implies piracy
23 *doxy* mistress of a ne'er-do-well
30 *states* estates

---

24 *John Leydens*. Ananias and Tribulation. Jan Bockelson of Leyden was
   one of the leaders of the Anabaptists at Munster (see II.v, 13), and many
   English Puritans found refuge in the town of Leyden itself.

DOL
   Yes, say lord General, how fares our camp?
FACE
   As, with the few, that had entrenched themselves
   Safe, by their discipline, against a world, Dol: 35
   And laughed, within those trenches, and grew fat
   With thinking on the booties, Dol, brought in
   Daily, by their small parties. This dear hour,
   A doughty don is taken, with my Dol;
   And thou may'st make his ransom, what thou wilt,   40
   My Dousabell: he shall be brought here, fettered
   With thy fair looks, before he sees thee; and thrown
   In a downbed, as dark as any dungeon;
   Where thou shalt keep him waking, with thy drum;
   Thy drum, my Dol; thy drum; till he be tame   45
   As the poor blackbirds were i' the great frost,
   Or bees are with a basin: and so hive him
   I' the swanskin coverlid, and cambric sheets,
   Till he work honey, and wax, my little God's-gift.
DOL
   What is he, General?
FACE   An adalantado,   50
   A grandee, girl. Was not my Dapper here, yet?
DOL
   No.
FACE   Nor my Drugger?
DOL   Neither.
FACE   A pox on 'em,
   They are so long a-furnishing! Such stinkards
   Would not be seen, upon these festival days.
                     [*Enter* SUBTLE]
   How now! Ha' you done?
SUBTLE   Done. They are gone. The sum   55
   Is here in bank, my Face. I would, we knew
   Another chapman, now, would buy 'em outright.

   33 *Yes, say lord General.* Dol quotes the opening line of Kyd's *Spanish
      Tragedy.*
   39 *taken* attracted by (punningly sustaining piratic image)
   44 *drum* (*cf.* line 22) bawdy innuendo. See *O.E.D.*
   46 *frost* of 1608
   49 *God's-gift* Greek meaning of Dorothy
   50 *adalantado* (loosely) Governor of a Province
   53 *a-furnishing* equipping themselves, preparing (to be gulled)
   54 *Would* probably with the force of *should*

   47 *Or bees are with a basin.* The sound of a metal basin being tapped attrac-
      ted bees. See Virgil, *Georgics*, 4.64.

FACE

  'Slid, Nab shall do't, against he ha' the widow,
  To furnish household.

SUBTLE   Excellent, well thought on,
  Pray God, he come.

FACE   I pray, he keep away   60
  Till our new business be o'erpast.

SUBTLE   But, Face,
  How camest thou, by this secret don?

FACE   A spirit
  Brought me th' intelligence, in a paper, here,
  As I was conjuring, yonder, in my circle
  For Surly: I ha' my flies abroad. Your bath   65
  Is famous, Subtle, by my means. Sweet Dol,
  You must go tune your virginal, no losing
  O' the least time. And, do you hear? Good action.
  Firk, like a flounder; kiss, like a scallop, close:
  And tickle him with thy mother-tongue. His great   70
  Verdugoship has not a jot of language:
  So much the easier to be cozened, my Dolly.
  He will come here, in a hired coach, obscure,
  And our own coachman, whom I have sent, as guide,
                        One knocks
  No creature else. Who's that?

SUBTLE   It i' not he?   75

FACE

  O no, not yet this hour.

SUBTLE   Who is't?

DOL   Dapper,
  Your clerk.

FACE   God's will, then, Queen of Fairy,
  On with your tire; and, Doctor, with your robes.
  Let's despatch him, for God's sake.

SUBTLE   'Twill be long.

FACE

  I warrant you, take but the cues I give you,   80

59 *furnish* provide (nearer to modern sense than at line 53)
64 *my circle* see III.iii, 2
66 *famous*, ed. (F, Q have no comma)
67–8 *tune . . . virginal . . . action* metaphor of preparing 16th century
    keyboard instrument for entertainment, with bawdy innuendo
69 *Firk* stir up (tr.) move about (intr.); *flounder* a small fish;
    scallop a shell-fish
71 *Verdugoship* verdugo is Spanish for executioner, used slangily;
    language i.e. English
73 *obscure* secretly, unobserved, unlike a grandee

It shall be brief enough. 'Slight, here are more!
Abel, and I think, the angry boy, the heir,
That fain would quarrel.
SUBTLE   And the widow?
FACE   No,
Not that I see. Away. O sir, you are welcome. [*Exit* SUBTLE]

Act III, Scene iv

[*Enter*] DAPPER

FACE

The Doctor is within, a-moving for you;
(I have had the most ado to win him to it)
He swears, you'll be the darling o' the dice:
He never heard her Highness dote, till now (he says.)
Your aunt has given you the most gracious words,   5
That can be thought on.
DAPPER   Shall I see her Grace?

[*Enter* DRUGGER *and* KASTRIL]

FACE

See her, and kiss her, too. What? Honest Nab!
Hast brought the damask?
DRUGGER   No, sir, here's tobacco.
FACE
'Tis well done, Nab: thou'lt bring the damask too?
DRUGGER
Yes, here's the gentleman, Captain, master Kastril,   10
I have brought to see the Doctor.
FACE   Where's the widow?
DRUGGER
Sir, as he likes, his sister (he says) shall come.
FACE
O, is it so? Good time. Is your name Kastril, sir?
KASTRIL
Ay, and the best o' the Kastrils, I'd be sorry else,
By fifteen hundred, a year. Where is this Doctor?   15
My mad tobacco-boy, here, tells me of one,
That can do things. Has he any skill?
FACE   Wherein, sir?

12 *as he likes* according to his wishes
13 *Good time* all in good time
14 i.e. his fortune outbids the rest by the sum named

KASTRIL

To carry a business, manage a quarrel, fairly,
Upon fit terms.

FACE   It seems sir, you're but young
About the town, that can make that a question!   20

KASTRIL

Sir, not so young, but I have heard some speech
Of the angry boys, and seen 'em take tobacco;
And in his shop: and I can take it too.
And I would fain be one of 'em, and go down
And practise i' the country.

FACE   Sir, for the *duello*,   25
The Doctor, I assure you, shall inform you,
To the least shadow of a hair; and show you,
An instrument he has, of his own making,
Wherewith, no sooner shall you make report
Of any quarrel, but he will take the height on't,   30
Most instantly; and tell in what degree,
Of safety it lies in, or mortality.
And, how it may be borne, whether in a right line,
Or a half-circle; or may, else, be cast
Into an angle blunt, if not acute: 35
All this he will demonstrate. And then, rules,
To give, and take the lie, by.

KASTRIL   How? To take it?

FACE

Yes, in oblique, he'll show you; or in circle:
But never in diameter. The whole town
Study his theorems, and dispute them, ordinarily,   40

18 *carry a business* duelling jargon   19 *fit* socially accepted
37 *and take* i.e. receive challenges
40 *ordinarily* punning on 'ordinaries', i.e. public houses of refresh-
ment; pun continued into line 41

---

22 *angry boys*. Sometimes called the 'roaring boys', these were young bucks
   who gained reputations for quarrels, assaults, and stylized thuggery.
   They have their counterparts in every century and society.
22 *take tobacco*. Abel's shop accommodated both the novice and the adept
   in the art of smoking. Here the adept practised the 'gulan ebolitio, the
   euripus, the whiff', and many other methods of retaining or emitting
   smoke.
25–39 *for the duello* &c. This collection of duelling jargon and punctilio is
   intended to 'blind with science'. The leading contemporary authority
   on the subject was *Vincentio Saviolo his Practise. In two Bookes. The first
   intreating of the use of the Rapier and Dagger. The second, of Honor and
   honorable Quarrels*, 1595. Cf. the degrees of the lie denominated by
   Touchstone in *As You Like It*, V.iv, and Fletcher's *The Queen of
   Corinth*, IV.i.

At the eating academies.

KASTRIL   But, does he teach
Living, by the wits, too?

FACE   Anything, whatever.
You cannot think that subtlety, but he reads it.
He made me a Captain. I was a stark pimp,
Just o' your standing, 'fore I met with him: 45
It i' not two months since. I'll tell you his method.
First, he will enter you, at some ordinary.

KASTRIL

No, I'll not come there. You shall pardon me.

FACE   For why, sir?

KASTRIL

There's gaming there, and tricks.

FACE   Why, would you be
A gallant, and not game?

KASTRIL   Ay, 'twill spend a man.   50

FACE

Spend you? It will repair you, when you are spent.
How do they live by their wits, there, that have vented
Six times your fortunes?

KASTRIL   What, three thousand a year!

FACE

Ay, forty thousand.

KASTRIL   Are there such?

FACE   Ay, sir.
And gallants, yet. Here's a young gentleman,   55
Is born to nothing, forty marks a year,
Which I count nothing. He's to be initiated,
And have a fly o' the Doctor. He will win you
By unresistable luck, within this fortnight,
Enough to buy a barony. They will set him   60
Upmost, at the Groom-porter's, all the Christmas!
And, for the whole year through, at every place,
Where there is play, present him with the chair;
The best attendance, the best drink, sometimes
Two glasses of canary, and pay nothing;   65
The purest linen, and the sharpest knife,
The partridge next his trencher: and, somewhere,
The dainty bed, in private, with the dainty.

44 *stark pimp* penniless go-between (pimp, with a less developed
   sense than now)
52 *vented* spent (ventured, adventured), made empty
61 *Groom-porter's* an officer of the royal household, especially concerned to regulate gaming

You shall ha' your ordinaries bid for him,
As playhouses for a poet; and the master   70
Pray him, aloud, to name what dish he affects,
Which must be buttered shrimps: and those that drink
To no mouth else, will drink to his, as being
The goodly, president mouth of all the board.

KASTRIL

Do you not gull one?

FACE   'Od's my life! Do you think it?   75
You shall have a cast commander, (can but get
In credit with a glover, or a spurrier,
For some two pair, of either's ware, aforehand)
Will, by most swift posts, dealing with him,
Arrive at competent means, to keep himself,   80
His punk, and naked boy, in excellent fashion.
And be admired for it.

KASTRIL   Will the Doctor teach this?

FACE

He will do more, sir, when your land is gone,
(As men of spirit hate to keep earth long)
In a vacation, when small money is stirring,   85
And ordinaries suspended till the term,
He'll show a perspective, where on one side
You shall behold the faces, and the persons
Of all sufficient young heirs, in town,
Whose bonds are current for commodity;   90
On th' other side, the merchants' forms, and others,
That, without help of any second broker,
(Who would expect a share) will trust such parcels:
In the third square, the very street, and sign
Where the commodity dwells, and does but wait   95
To be delivered, be it pepper, soap,
Hops, or tobacco, oatmeal, woad, or cheeses.
All which you may so handle, to enjoy,
To your own use, and never stand obliged.

KASTRIL

I' faith! Is he such a fellow?

---

76 *cast* cashiered   77 *spurrier* spur maker
78 i.e. once he can obtain advance of goods
79 *swift posts* with speed in delivery and exchange, like post-horses
85 *vacation* i.e. from law terms   90 *current* at present in the market
93 *parcels* i.e. of goods   97 *woad* plant yielding blue dye

---

87 *perspective.* A specially devised optical instrument, or, perhaps primarily,
  a design constructed to produce remarkable effects. See *O.E.D.*
90 *commodity.* See note to II.i, 10–14.

FACE   Why, Nab here knows him.   100
And then for making matches, for rich widows,
Young gentlewomen, heirs, the fortunat'st man!
He's sent to, far, and near, all over England,
To have his counsel, and to know their fortunes.

KASTRIL
God's will, my suster shall see him.

FACE   I'll tell you, sir,   105
What he did tell me of Nab. It's a strange thing!
(By the way you must eat no cheese, Nab, it breeds melan-
                                                    choly:
And that same melancholy breeds worms) but pass it–
He told me, honest Nab, here, was ne'er at tavern,
But once in's life.

DRUGGER   Truth, and no more I was not.   110

FACE
And, then he was so sick—

DRUGGER   Could he tell you that, too?

FACE
How should I know it?

DRUGGER   In troth we had been a-shooting,
And had a piece of fat ram-mutton, to supper,
That lay so heavy o' my stomach—

FACE   And he has no head
To bear any wine; for, what with the noise o' the fiddlers,   115
And care of his shop, for he dares keep no servants—

DRUGGER
My head did so ache—

FACE   As he was fain to be brought home,
The Doctor told me. And then, a good old woman—

DRUGGER
(Yes, faith, she dwells in Sea-coal Lane) did cure me,
With sodden ale, and pellitory o' the wall: 120
Cost me but two pence. I had another sickness,
Was worse than that.

---

104 *and to know* i.e. by those who wish to know
105 *suster* sister; intended to suggest rustic dialect
108 *pass it* let it pass
112 *How should* how else should
119 *Sea-coal Lane* a lane between Snow Hill and Fleet Street
120 *pellitory* the wall-pellitory, a plant used to prepare demulcents and
     emollients

---

107 *breeds melancholy*. 'Milk, and all that comes of milk, as butter and
cheese, curds, &c., increase melancholy'. Burton, *Anatomy of Melancholy*, part 1, sec. 2, mem. 2, subs. 1.

FACE   Ay, that was with the grief
   Thou took'st for being 'sessed at eighteen pence,
   For the water-work.
DRUGGER   In truth, and it was like
   T'have cost me almost my life.
FACE   Thy hair went off?   **125**
DRUGGER
   Yes, sir, 'twas done for spite.
FACE   Nay, so says the Doctor.
KASTRIL
   Pray thee, tobacco-boy, go fetch my suster,
   I'll see this learned boy, before I go:
   And so shall she.
FACE   Sir, he is busy now:
   But, if you have a sister to fetch hither,   **130**
   Perhaps, your own pains may command her sooner;
   And he, by that time, will be free.
KASTRIL   I go.   [*Exit* KASTRIL]
FACE
   Drugger, she's thine: the damask. (Subtle, and I
                              [*Exit* DRUGGER]
   Must wrestle for her.) Come on, master Dapper.
   You see, how I turn clients, here, away,   **135**
   To give your cause despatch. Ha' you performed
   The ceremonies were enjoined you?
DAPPER   Yes, o' the vinegar,
   And the clean shirt.
FACE   'Tis well: that shirt may do you
   More worship than you think. Your aunt's afire
   But that she will not show it, t'have a sight on you.   **140**
   Ha' you provided for her Grace's servants?
DAPPER
   Yes, here are six score Edward shillings.
FACE   Good.
DAPPER
   And an old Harry's sovereign.
FACE   Very good.
DAPPER
   And three James shillings, and an Elizabeth groat,

123 *'sessed* assessed
132 *I go* so F (Q has *I go, sir*)
143 *old Harry's sovereign* debased currency: worth ten shillings

---

124 *the water-work.* Sir Hugh Myddleton's New River, begun in 1609 and
      completed in 1613.

Just twenty nobles.

FACE   O, you are too just.   145

I would you had had the other noble in Marys.

DAPPER

I have some Philip, and Marys.

FACE   Ay, those same

Are best of all. Where are they? Hark, the Doctor.

Act III, Scene v

[*Enter*] SUBTLE

SUBTLE

Is yet her Grace's cousin come?   SUBTLE *disguised like a*
                                          Priest of Fairy

FACE   He is come.

SUBTLE

And is he fasting?

FACE   Yes.

SUBTLE   And hath cried *hum*?

FACE

Thrice, you must answer.

DAPPER   Thrice.

SUBTLE   And as oft *buz*?

FACE

If you have, say.

DAPPER   I have.

SUBTLE   Then, to her coz,

Hoping, that he hath vinegared his senses,   5

As he was bid, the Fairy Queen dispenses,

By me, this robe, the petticoat of Fortune;

Which that he straight put on, she doth importune.

And though to Fortune near be her petticoat,

Yet, nearer is her smock, the Queen doth note: 10

And, therefore, even of that a piece she hath sent,

Which, being a child, to wrap him in, was rent;

---

4 *coz* cousin, (any close or distant kin)
8 *importune* beg, request
10 (proverbial) *cf.* 'Though ny be my kyrtell, yet nere is my smock' (HS)
12 *being a* i.e. when he was yet a

---

145 *twenty nobles.* (at six shillings and eightpence each) £6 13s 4d Dapper's totalling is accurate. The 'Marys' (line 146) are to fill the gap in successive reigns. Face's numismatics divert attention from the money itself.

And prays him, for a scarf, he now will wear it
They blind him with a rag
(With as much love, as then her Grace did tear it)
About his eyes, to show, he is fortunate.   15
And, trusting unto her to make his state,
He'll throw away all worldly pelf, about him;
Which that he will perform, she doth not doubt him.

FACE

She need not doubt him, sir. Alas, he has nothing,
But what he will part withall, as willingly,   20
Upon her Grace's word (throw away your purse)
As she would ask it: (handkerchiefs, and all)
She cannot bid that thing, but he'll obey.
(If you have a ring, about you, cast it off,
Or a silver seal, at your wrist, her Grace will send   25
He throws away, as they bid him
Her fairies here to search you, therefore deal
Directly with her Highness. If they find
That you conceal a mite, you are undone.)

DAPPER

Truly, there's all.

FACE   All what?

DAPPER   My money, truly.

FACE

Keep nothing, that is transitory, about you.   30
(Bid Dol play music.) Look, the elves are come
Dol enters with a cithern: they pinch him
To pinch you, if you tell not truth. Advise you.

DAPPER

O, I have a paper with a spur-rial in't.

FACE   *Ti, ti,*
They knew't, they say.

SUBTLE   *Ti, ti, ti, ti,* he has more yet.

FACE

Ti, ti-ti-ti. I' the t'other pocket?

SUBTLE   *Titi, titi, titi, titi.*   35
They must pinch him, or he will never confess, they say.

DAPPER

O, O.

FACE   Nay, pray you hold. He is her Grace's nephew.

---

16 *state* high rank, status, wealth
17 *pelf* money, jewellery, valuable gear
27 *Directly* frankly, honourably
31 *cithern* (or cittern) species of guitar. Cf. Tyrolean Zither
33 *spur-rial* Edward IV noble, value about fifteen shillings

Ti, ti, ti? What care you? Good faith, you shall care.
Deal plainly, sir, and shame the fairies. Show
You are an innocent.
DAPPER   By this good light, I ha' nothing.   40
SUBTLE
Ti ti, ti ti to ta. He does equivocate, she says:
Ti, ti do ti, ti ti do, ti da. And swears by the light, when he
                                                  is blinded.
DAPPER
By this good dark, I ha' nothing but a half crown
Of gold, about my wrist, that my love gave me;
And a leaden heart I wore, sin' she forsook me.   45
FACE
I thought, 'twas something. And, would you incur
Your aunt's displeasure for these trifles? Come,
I had rather you had thrown away twenty half crowns.
You may wear your leaden heart still. How now?
SUBTLE
What news, Dol?
DOL   Yonder's your knight, sir Mammon.   50
FACE
God's lid, we never thought of him, till now.
Where is he?
DOL   Here, hard by. He's at the door.
SUBTLE
And, you are not ready, now? Dol, get his suit.
He must not be sent back.
FACE   O, by no means.
What shall we do with this same puffin, here,   55
Now he's o' the spit?
SUBTLE   Why, lay him back a while,
With some device. *Ti, ti ti, ti ti ti.* Would her Grace speak
                                                  with me?

I come. Help, Dol.
FACE   Who's there? Sir Epicure;
He speaks through the keyhole, the other knocking
My master's i' the way. Please you to walk
Three or four turns, but till his back be turned,   60
And I am for you. Quickly, Dol.
SUBTLE   Her Grace

---

40 *innocent* (ironically playing on both senses)
43 *half crown/Of gold* first coined in Henry VIII's reign
53 *his suit* i.e. Face's costume for the role of servant
55 *puffin* derisive term for a puffed-up 'gull'; the Didapper was a
   near-species, in Elizabethan ornithology

    Commends her kindly to you, master Dapper.

DAPPER

    I long to see her Grace.

SUBTLE   She, now, is set

    At dinner, in her bed; and she has sent you,

    From her own private trencher, a dead mouse,   65

    And a piece of gingerbread, to be merry withal,

    And stay your stomach, lest you faint with fasting:

    Yet, if you could hold out, till she saw you (she says)

    It would be better for you.

FACE   Sir, he shall

    Hold out, and 'twere this two hours, for her Highness;   70

    I can assure you that. We will not lose

    All we ha' done—

SUBTLE   He must nor see, nor speak

    To anybody, till then.

FACE   For that, we'll put, sir,

    A stay in 's mouth.

SUBTLE   Of what?

FACE   Of gingerbread.

    Make you it fit. He that hath pleased her Grace,   75

    Thus far, shall not now crinkle, for a little.

    Gape sir, and let him fit you.

SUBTLE   Where shall we now

    Bestow him?

DOL   I' the privy.

SUBTLE   Come along, sir,

    I now must show you Fortune's privy lodgings.

FACE

    Are they perfumed? And his bath ready?

SUBTLE   All.   80

    Only the fumigation's somewhat strong.

FACE

    Sir Epicure, I am yours, sir, by and by.   *[Exeunt]*

Act IV, Scene i

[Enter] FACE, MAMMON

FACE

    O, sir, you're come i' the only, finest time—

MAMMON

    Where's master?

74 *stay* gag
76 *crinkle* curl away, recoil, shrink
 1 *only* (onely) singularly, uniquely

FACE   Now preparing for projection, sir.
  Your stuff will b' all changed shortly.
MAMMON   Into gold?
FACE
  To gold, and silver, sir.
MAMMON   Silver, I care not for.
FACE
  Yes, sir, a little to give beggars.
MAMMON   Where's the lady?   5
FACE
  At hand, here. I ha' told her such brave things, o' you,
  Touching your bounty and your noble spirit—
MAMMON   Hast thou?
FACE
  As she is almost in her fit to see you.
  But, good sir, no divinity i' your conference,
  For fear of putting her in rage—
MAMMON   I warrant thee.   10
FACE
  Six men will not hold her down. And, then,
  If the old man should hear, or see you—
MAMMON   Fear not.
FACE
  The very house, sir, would run mad. You know it
  How scrupulous he is, and violent,
  'Gainst the least act of sin. Physic, or mathematics,   15
  Poetry, state, or bawdry (as I told you)
  She will endure, and never startle: but
  No word of controversy.
MAMMON   I am schooled, good Eulen.
FACE
  And you must praise her house, remember that,
  And her nobility.
MAMMON   Let me, alone: 20
  No Herald, no nor Antiquary, Lungs,
  Shall do it better. Go.
FACE   Why, this is yet
  A kind of modern happiness, to have
  Dol Common for a great lady.
MAMMON   Now, Epicure,
  Heighten thyself, talk to her, all in gold;   25

14 *scrupulous* piously conscientious, *plus* attentive to detail
23 *modern* ordinary, common (punning on her name) as well as
   fashionable, modish; *happiness* includes the sense fitness, aptness

Rain her as many showers, as Jove did drops
Unto his Danae: show the God a miser,
Compared with Mammon. What? The stone will do't.
She shall feel gold, taste gold, hear gold, sleep gold:
Nay, we will *concumbere* gold. I will be puissant,   30
And mighty in my talk to her! Here she comes.

[*Enter* DOL]

FACE
To him, Dol, suckle him. This is the noble knight,
I told your ladyship—
MAMMON   Madam, with your pardon,
I kiss your vesture.
DOL   Sir, I were uncivil
If I would suffer that, my lip to you, sir.   35
MAMMON
I hope, my lord your brother be in health, lady?
DOL
My lord, my brother is, though I no lady, sir.
FACE
(Well said my Guinea bird.)
MAMMON   Right noble madam—
FACE
(O, we shall have most fierce idolatry!)
MAMMON
'Tis your prerogative.
DOL   Rather your courtesy.   40
MAMMON
Were there nought else t'enlarge your virtues, to me,
These answers speak your breeding, and your blood.
DOL
Blood we boast none, sir, a poor baron's daughter.
MAMMON
Poor! And gat you? Profane not. Had your father
Slept all the happy remnant of his life   45
After that act, lain but there still, and panted,
He'd done enough, to make himself, his issue,
And his posterity noble.
DOL   Sir, although
We may be said to want the gilt, and trappings,
The dress of honour; yet we strive to keep   50
The seeds, and the materials.

30 *concumbere* breed, lying together
38 *Guinea bird* guinea-hen was slang for prostitute
44 *gat* begat

MAMMON   I do see
  The old ingredient, virtue, was not lost,
  Nor the drug money, used to make your compound.
  There is a strange nobility, i' your eye,
  This lip, that chin! Methinks you do resemble   55
  One o' the Austriac princes.
FACE   (Very like,
  Her father was an Irish costermonger.)
MAMMON
  The house of Valois, just, had such a nose.
  And such a forehead, yet, the Medici
  Of Florence boast.
DOL   Troth, and I have been likened   60
  To all these princes.
FACE   (I'll be sworn, I heard it.)
MAMMON
  I know not how. It is not any one,
  But e'en the very choice of all their features.
FACE
  (I'll in, and laugh.)   [*Exit* FACE]
MAMMON   A certain touch, or air,
  That sparkles a divinity, beyond   65
  An earthly beauty!
DOL   O, you play the courtier.
MAMMON
  Good lady, gi' me leave—
DOL   In faith, I may not,
  To mock me, sir.
MAMMON   To burn i' this sweet flame:
  The Phoenix never knew a nobler death.
DOL
  Nay, now you court the courtier: and destroy   70
  What you would build. This art, sir, i' your words,
  Calls your whole faith in question.
MAMMON   By my soul—

53 Mammon turns even his compliments alchemically
56 *Austriac* Austrian
57 *Irish* (as all costermongers were colloquially said to be)
70 *court* seek to be, mimic
71 *art* i.e. decorative, mannered; with suggestion of guile

56 *the Austriac princes*. '. . . The *Austrian* Lip at this day is by good right
  in high esteem; it being observed, that all the House of *Austria* have a
  sweet fulnesse of the Nether lip'. John Bulwer, *Anthropometamorphosis*,
  1650, p. 106. The Valois nose and the Medici forehead which follow
  (lines 58, 59) are Jonson's joke; neither feature is distinctive in those
  families (Herford and Simpson).

DOL

Nay, oaths are made o' the same air, sir.

MAMMON   Nature

Never bestowed upon mortality,
A more unblamed, a more harmonious feature: 75
She played the stepdame in all faces, else.
Sweet madam, le' me be particular—

DOL

Particular, sir? I pray you, know your distance.

MAMMON

In no ill sense, sweet lady, but to ask
How your fair graces pass the hours? I see   80
You're lodged, here, i' the house of a rare man,
An excellent artist: but, what's that to you?

DOL

Yes, sir. I study here the mathematics,
And distillation.

MAMMON   O, I cry your pardon.

He's a divine instructor! Can extract   85
The souls of all things, by his art; call all
The virtues, and the miracles of the sun,
Into a temperate furnace: teach dull nature
What her own forces are. A man, the Emperor
Has courted, above Kelley: sent his medals,   90
And chains, t' invite him.

DOL   Ay, and for his physic, sir—

MAMMON

Above the art of Æsculapius,
That drew the envy of the Thunderer!
I know all this, and more.

75 *feature* form, proportions, shape, composition
76 *else* i.e. in all other faces
77 *particular* intimate, private, personal
80 i.e. the person who gathers these graces to herself
82 *artist* here, practiser of the secret arts, the mysteries
83 *mathematics* astrology (essentially)
84 *distillation* chemistry (essentially)
88 *temperate* controlled, regulated
89 *Emperor* Rudolph II of Germany

---

90 *Kelley*. Edward Kelley (1555–95), the partner of John Dee, was an ener-
    getic man who procured the favour of Rudolph II by boasting that he
    possessed the philosopher's stone. Rudolph twice imprisoned him to
    force him into some action. On the second occasion Kelley attempted
    escape and was killed.
92 *Æsculapius*. The god, or 'patron saint' of the doctors, who restored men
    to life until Zeus (the Thunderer) killed him with a flash of lightning,
    lest men should escape death altogether.

DOL   Troth, I am taken, sir,
  Whole, with these studies, that contemplate nature: 95
MAMMON
  It is a noble humour. But, this form
  Was not intended to so dark a use!
  Had you been crooked, foul, of some coarse mould,
  A cloister had done well: but, such a feature
  That might stand up the glory of a kingdom,   100
  To live recluse! Is a mere solecism,
  Though in a nunnery. It must not be.
  I muse, my lord your brother will permit it!
  You should spend half my land first, were I he.
  Does not this diamond better, on my finger,   105
  Than i' the quarry?
DOL   Yes.
MAMMON   Why, you are like it.
  You were created, lady, for the light!
  Here, you shall wear it; take it, the first pledge
  Of what I speak: to bind you, to believe me.
DOL
  In chains of adamant?
MAMMON   Yes, the strongest bands.   110
  And take a secret, too. Here, by your side,
  Doth stand, this hour, the happiest man, in Europe.
DOL
  You are contented, sir?
MAMMON   Nay, in true being:
  The envy of princes, and the fear of states.
DOL
  Say you so, Sir Epicure!
MAMMON   Yes, and thou shalt prove it,   115
  Daughter of honour. I have cast mine eye
  Upon thy form, and I will rear this beauty,
  Above all styles.
DOL   You mean no treason, sir!

  95 *Whole* wholly
  96 *this form* i.e. her person
 101 *solecism* incongruity, quite unfitting
 102 *Though* even if, although it be
 103 *muse* am bemused, astonished
 109 *speak* shall now say
 110 *adamant* punning on old form of diamond, then in use: diamant;
    bands bonds
 112 *happiest* (beatus) wealthiest, as well as happiest
 118 *styles* fashions of beauty, cults (glancing, perhaps, at the older
    meaning, engravings)

MAMMON
  No, I will take away that jealousy.
  I am the lord of the philosopher's stone,   120
  And thou the lady.
DOL   How sir! Ha' you that?
MAMMON
  I am the master of the mastery.
  This day, the good old wretch, here, o' the house
  Has made it for us. Now, he's at projection.
  Think therefore, thy first wish, now; let me hear it: 125
  And it shall rain into thy lap, no shower,
  But floods of gold, whole cataracts, a deluge,
  To get a nation on thee!
DOL   You are pleased, sir,
  To work on the ambition of our sex.
MAMMON
  I am pleased, the glory of her sex should know,   130
  This nook, here, of the Friars, is no climate
  For her, to live obscurely in, to learn
  Physic, and surgery, for the Constable's wife
  Of some odd Hundred in Essex; but come forth,
  And taste the air of palaces; eat, drink   135
  The toils of empirics, and their boasted practice;
  Tincture of pearl, and coral, gold, and amber;
  Be seen at feasts, and triumphs; have it asked,
  What miracle she is? Set all the eyes
  Of court afire, like a burning glass,   140
  And work 'em into cinders; when the jewels
  Of twenty states adorn thee; and the light
  Strikes out the stars; that, when thy name is mentioned,
  Queens may look pale: and, we but showing our love,
  Nero's Poppæa may be lost in story!   145

119 *jealousy* suspicion
126 as in the myth of Danae (HS)
131 *the Friars* i.e. Blackfriars (with glancing pun, perhaps)

---

122 *the mastery*. The *magisterium*, the mystery of the stone, the master-
    touch. The word also carries its older sense of 'mystery' or 'trade'. Cf.
    Abhorson on the executioner's trade in *Measure for Measure*, IV.ii:
    'A bawd, sir? Fie upon him; he will discredit our mystery'.
136 *empirics*. An empiric is literally one who makes experiments, but the
    word had come to mean a quack: cf. Burton. *Anatomy of Melancholy*,
    part 2, sec. 1, mem. 4, subs. 1 'There be many Mountebanks, Quack-
    salvers, Empiricks, in every street'.
145 *Nero's Poppæa*. Mammon calls to mind the legendary splendour and
    luxury of their amour. It was said that she was so anxious to preserve
    her beauty that five hundred asses were kept to provide the milk in
    which she used daily to bathe. But see *Oxford Classical Dictionary*.

Thus, will we have it.
DOL   I could well consent, sir.
But, in a monarchy, how will this be?
The Prince will soon take notice; and both seize
You, and your stone: it being a wealth unfit
For any private subject.
MAMMON   If he knew it.   150
DOL
Yourself do boast it, sir.
MAMMON   To thee, my life.
DOL
O, but beware, sir! You may come to end
The remnant of your days, in a loathed prison,
By speaking of it.
MAMMON   'Tis no idle fear!
We'll therefore go with all, my girl, and live   155
In a free state; where we will eat our mullets,
Soused in high-country wines, sup pheasants' eggs,
And have our cockles, boiled in silver shells,
Our shrimps to swim again, as when they lived,
In a rare butter, made of dolphins' milk,   160
Whose cream does look like opals: and, with these
Delicate meats, set ourselves high for pleasure,
And take us down again, and then renew
Our youth, and strength, with drinking the elixir,
And so enjoy a perpetuity   165
Of life, and lust. And, thou shalt ha' thy wardrobe,
Richer than nature's, still, to change thyself,
And vary oftener, for thy pride, than she:
Or art, her wise, and almost equal servant.

[*Enter* FACE]

FACE
Sir, you are too loud. I hear you, every word,   170
Into the laboratory. Some fitter place.
The garden, or great chamber above. How like you her?
MAMMON
Excellent! Lungs. There's for thee.
FACE   But, do you hear?
Good sir, beware, no mention of the Rabbins.

148–50 several vouched-for cases could be cited
156 *mullets* fish; a reputed delicacy of Roman feasting
160 *dolphins' milk* (both rare, and rich)
171 *Into* i.e. right through into
174 *Rabbins* Rabbis, especially the more learned

MAMMON
  We think not on 'em.

[Exeunt DOL, MAMMON]

FACE   O, it is well, sir. Subtle!   175

Act IV, Scene ii

[*Enter*] SUBTLE

FACE
  Dost thou not laugh?
SUBTLE   Yes. Are they gone?
FACE   All's clear.
SUBTLE
  The widow is come.
FACE   And your quarrelling disciple?
SUBTLE
  Ay.
FACE   I must to my Captainship again, then.
SUBTLE
  Stay, bring 'em in, first.
FACE   So I meant. What is she?
  A bonnibell?
SUBTLE   I know not.
FACE   We'll draw lots,   5
  You'll stand to that?
SUBTLE   What else?
FACE   O, for a suit,
  To fall now, like a curtain: flap.
SUBTLE   To th' door, man.
FACE
  You'll ha' the first kiss, 'cause I am not ready.

[Exit FACE]

SUBTLE
  Yes, and perhaps hit you through both the nostrils.
FACE [*within*]
  Who would you speak with?
KASTRIL [*within*]   Where's the Captain?

---

3 *Captainship* i.e. the appropriate costume
5 *bonnibell* colloquial (rustic) term of endearment for a Beauty
7 *flap* a term to mime the sudden 'arrival' of the uniform

---

9 *through both the nostrils*. Probably 'lead you by the nose'. See *Isaiah*,
xxxvii, 29, and cf. *Othello*, I.iii 'And will as tenderly be led by the nose
as asses are'.

FACE   Gone, sir.   10
  About some business.
KASTRIL   Gone?
FACE   He'll return straight.
  But master Doctor, his lieutenant, is here.
        [*Enter* KASTRIL, DAME PLIANT]
SUBTLE
  Come near, my worshipful boy, my *terrae fili*,
  That is, my boy of land; make thy approaches:
  Welcome, I know thy lusts, and thy desires,   15
  And I will serve, and satisfy 'em.
  Charge me from thence, or thence, or in this line;
  Here is my centre: ground thy quarrel.
KASTRIL   You lie.
SUBTLE
  How, child of wrath, and anger! The loud lie?
  For what, my sudden boy?
KASTRIL   Nay, that look you to,   20
  I am aforehand.
SUBTLE   O, this 's no true grammar,
  And as ill logic! You must render causes, child,
  Your first, and second intentions, know your canons,
  And your divisions, moods, degrees, and differences,
  Your predicaments, substance, and accident,   25
  Series extern, and intern, with their causes
  Efficient, material, formal, final,
  And ha' your elements perfect—
KASTRIL   What is this!
  The angry tongue he talks in?
SUBTLE   That false precept,
  Of being aforehand, has deceived a number;   30
  And made 'em enter quarrels, oftentimes,
  Before they were aware: and, afterward,
  Against their wills.
KASTRIL   How must I do then, sir?

---

13 *terrae fili* landed proprietor; but the term also had a colloquial sig-
    nificance – man of mean birth
17 resuming Face's geometrical jargon for duelling punctilio
20 *sudden* impetuous
21 *aforehand* made the first move; *grammar* from this point Subtle
    deploys the terms of scholastic argument to constitute a fresh
    pseudo-science of duelling punctilio
23 *canons* general axioms
25 *predicaments* what is predicated or asserted (in technical argument)
28 *elements* first principles
29 *angry* i.e. baffling, and also relating to quarrel-techniques

SUBTLE

    I cry this lady mercy. She should, first,
Have been saluted. I do call you lady,   35
Because you are to be one, ere 't be long,
He kisses her
My soft, and buxom widow.

KASTRIL   Is she, i'faith?

SUBTLE

    Yes, or my art is an egregious liar.

KASTRIL

    How know you?

SUBTLE   By inspection, on her forehead,
And subtlety of her lip, which must be tasted   40
He kisses her again
Often, to make a judgement. 'Slight, she melts
Like a myrobalan! Here is, yet, a line
In *rivo frontis*, tells me, he is no knight.

PLIANT

    What is he then, sir?

SUBTLE   Let me see your hand.
O, your *linea Fortunae* makes it plain;   45
And *stella* here, in *monte Veneris*:
But, most of all, *iunctura annularis*.
He is a soldier, or a man of art, lady:
But shall have some great honour, shortly.

PLIANT   Brother,
He's a rare man, believe me!

KASTRIL   Hold your peace.   50
[*Enter* FACE]
Here comes the tother rare man. Save you Captain.

FACE

    Good master Kastril. Is this your sister?

KASTRIL   Ay, sir.
Please you to kuss her, and be proud to know her?

FACE

    I shall be proud to know you, lady.

---

38 *egregious* gross, conspicuous
40 *subtlety* (carries a lascivious intention) a refined species of confectionery
42 *myrobalan* a sweetmeat   43 *rivo frontis* the frontal vein (HS)
45 *linea Fortunae* the line of fortune, in palmistry, runs from beneath the little finger towards the index finger
46 *stella* a star on the hill of Venus (at the root of the thumb): equivocal terminology
47 *iunctura* the joint of the ring finger
54 *know* (used equivocally)

PLIANT   Brother,
  He calls me lady, too.
KASTRIL   Ay, peace. I heard it.   55
FACE
  The Count is come.
SUBTLE   Where is he?
FACE   At the door.
SUBTLE
  Why, you must entertain him.
FACE   What'll you do
  With these the while?
SUBTLE   Why, have 'em up, and show 'em
  Some fustian book, or the dark glass.
FACE   'Fore God,
  She is a delicate dab-chick! I must have her.   60

                                     [*Exit* FACE]

SUBTLE
  Must you? Ay, if your fortune will, you must.
  Come sir, the Captain will come to us presently.
  I'll ha' you to my chamber of demonstrations,
  Where I'll show you both the grammar, and logic,
  And rhetoric of quarrelling; my whole method,   65
  Drawn out in tables; and my instrument,
  That hath the several scale upon't, shall make you
  Able to quarrel, at a straw's breadth, by moonlight.
  And, lady, I'll have you look in a glass,
  Some half an hour, but to clear your eyesight,   70
  Against you see your fortune: which is greater,
  Than I may judge upon the sudden, trust me.
                   [*Exeunt* SUBTLE, KASTRIL, PLIANT]

Act IV, Scene iii

[*Enter*] FACE

FACE
  Where are you, Doctor?
SUBTLE [*within*]   I'll come to you presently.
FACE
  I will ha' this same widow, now I ha' seen her,
  On any composition.

59 *fustian* bombastic, jargon-laden
60 *dab-chick* little grebe, 'hence a synonym for daintiness' (HS)
67 *several* divided up, partitioned
71 *Against* in preparation for
 3 *composition* barter arrangement, agreement

[*Enter* SUBTLE]

SUBTLE   What do you say?
FACE
  Ha' you disposed of them?
SUBTLE   I ha' sent 'em up.
FACE
  Subtle, in troth, I needs must have this widow.   5
SUBTLE
  Is that the matter?
FACE   Nay, but hear me.
SUBTLE   Go to,
  If you rebel once, Dol shall know it all.
  Therefore be quiet, and obey your chance.
FACE
  Nay, thou art so violent now—Do but conceive:
  Thou art old, and canst not serve—
SUBTLE   Who, cannot, I?   10
  'Slight, I will serve her with thee, for a—
FACE   Nay,
  But understand: I'll gi' you composition.
SUBTLE
  I will not treat with thee: what, sell my fortune?
  'Tis better than my birthright. Do not murmur.
  Win her, and carry her. If you grumble, Dol   15
  Knows it directly.
FACE   Well sir, I am silent.
  Will you go help, to fetch in Don, in state?   [*Exit* FACE]
SUBTLE
  I follow you, sir: we must keep Face in awe,
  Or he will overlook us like a tyrant.

              [*Enter* FACE,] SURLY *like a Spaniard*

  Brain of a tailor! Who comes here? Don John!   20
SURLY
  Señores, beso las manos, á vuestras mercedes.
SUBTLE
  Would you had stooped a little, and kissed our *anos.*
FACE
  Peace Subtle.
SUBTLE   Stab me; I shall never hold, man.

  10 *serve* (used equivocally)
  15 *and carry* and then take, after winning
  17 *state* in style
  21 i.e. I kiss your hands, gentlemen
  23 i.e. Let me blood: I shall burst

He looks in that deep ruff, like a head in a platter,
Served in by a short cloak upon two trestles!   25
FACE
  Or, what do you say to a collar of brawn, cut down
  Beneath the souse, and wriggled with a knife?
SUBTLE
  'Slud, he does look too fat to be a Spaniard.
FACE
  Perhaps some Fleming, or some Hollander got him
  In d'Alva's time: Count Egmont's bastard.
SUBTLE   Don,   30
  Your scurvy, yellow, Madrid face is welcome.
SURLY
  Gratia.
SUBTLE   He speaks, out of a fortification.
  Pray God, he ha' no squibs in those deep sets.
SURLY
  Por Dios, Señores, muy linda casa!
SUBTLE
  What says he?
FACE   Praises the house, I think,   35
  I know no more but's action.
SUBTLE   Yes, the *casa*,
  My precious Diego, will prove fair enough,
  To cozen you in. Do you mark? You shall
  Be cozened, Diego.
FACE   Cozened, do you see?
  My worthy Donzel, cozened.
SURLY   *Entiendo.*   40
SUBTLE
  Do you intend it? So do we, dear Don.
  Have you brought pistolets? Or portagues?
                    He feels his pockets

25 instead of servers and legs
27 *souse* ears (of pig)
32 *Gratia* Thanks; *fortification* see previous mock analogies.
    Enormous Spanish ruffs were a frequent occasion of jests
33 *sets* plaits, or folds of ruff
34 'Fore God, gentlemen, a very fine house
37 *Diego* (James) English 'name' for a Spaniard, applied at random
40 *Donzel* (Italian) squire; *Entiendo* I understand

29–30 *Perhaps some Fleming* &c. Netherlanders were proverbially fat.
   Fernando Alvarez, Duke of Alva, was governor of the Netherlands
   from 1567 to 1573. Lamoral, Count of Egmont, was a Flemish patriot
   executed by Alva in 1568.

My solemn Don? Dost thou feel any?

FACE   Full.

SUBTLE

   You shall be emptied, Don; pumped, and drawn,
   Dry, as they say.

FACE   Milked, in troth, sweet Don.   45

SUBTLE

   See all the monsters; the great lion of all, Don.

SURLY

   Con licencia, se puede ver á esta señora?

SUBTLE

   What talks he now?

FACE   O' the *Señora.*

SUBTLE   O, Don,

   That is the lioness, which you shall see
   Also, my Don.

FACE   'Slid, Subtle, how shall we do?   50

SUBTLE

   For what?

FACE   Why, Dol's employed, you know.

SUBTLE   That's true!

   'Fore heaven I know not: he must stay, that's all.

FACE

   Stay? That he must not by no means.

SUBTLE   No, why?

FACE

   Unless you'll mar all. 'Slight, he'll suspect it.
   And then he will not pay, not half so well.   55
   This is a travelled punk-master, and does know
   All the delays: a notable hot rascal,
   And looks, already, rampant.

SUBTLE   'Sdeath, and Mammon

   Must not be troubled.

FACE   Mammon, in no case!

SUBTLE

   What shall we do then?

FACE   Think: you must be sudden.   60

SURLY

   *Entiendo, que la señora es tan hermosa, que codicio tan
   á verla, como la bien aventuranza de mi vida.*

FACE

   Mi vida? 'Slid, Subtle, he puts me in mind o' the widow.

47 With your permission, may I see the lady?
61 I understand that the lady is so beautiful, that I am as eager to
   see her, as for whatever good fortune life brings

What dost thou say to draw her to't? Ha?
And tell her, it is her fortune. All our venture   65
Now lies upon 't. It is but one man more,
Which on's chance to have her: and, beside,
There is no maidenhead, to be feared, or lost.
What dost thou think on 't, Subtle?

SUBTLE   Who, I? Why—

FACE

The credit of our house too is engaged.   70

SUBTLE

You made me an offer for my share erewhile.
What wilt thou gi' me, i'faith?

FACE   O, by that light,
I'll not buy now. You know your doom to me.
E'en take your lot, obey your chance, sir; win her,
And wear her, out for me.

SUBTLE   'Slight. I'll not work her then.   75

FACE

It is the common cause, therefore bethink you.
Dol else must know it, as you said.

SUBTLE   I care not.

SURLY

Señores, por qué se tarda tanto?

SUBTLE

Faith, I am not fit, I am old.

FACE   That's now no reason, sir.

SURLY

Puede ser, de hacer burla de mi amor?   80

FACE

You hear the Don, too? By this air, I call.
And loose the hinges, Dol.

SUBTLE   A plague of hell—

FACE

Will you then do?

SUBTLE   You're a terrible rogue,
I'll think of this: will you, sir, call the widow?

65 *venture* undertaking, risk, investment   66 *lies* hangs
67 *Which on's* whichever of us's chance it is   73 *doom* lot, fate
78 Why is there so much delay, sirs?; *tanto* F, Q have *tanta*,
    perhaps indicating current pronunciation
80 Is it possible you are mocking at my love?
82 i.e. I will give the game away, and loudly

74–75 *win her, And wear her, out.* Face is probably glancing at the pro-
    verbial 'Win her and wear her' (of a man and his bride) and turning it
    coarsely.

FACE
> Yes, and I'll take her too, with all her faults,   85
> Now I do think on't better.

SUBTLE   With all my heart, sir,
> Am I discharged o' the lot?

FACE   As you please.

SUBTLE   Hands.

FACE
> Remember now, that upon any change,
> You never claim her.

SUBTLE   Much good joy, and health to you, sir.
> Marry a whore? Fate, let me wed a witch first.   90

SURLY
> *Por estas honradas barbas—*

SUBTLE   He swears by his beard.
> Despath, and call the brother too.   [*Exit* FACE]

SURLY   *Tengo dúda, Señores,*
> *Que no me hágan alguna traición.*

SUBTLE
> How, issue on? Yes, *presto Señor*. Please you
> *Enthratha* the *chambratha*, worthy Don;   95
> Where if it please the Fates, in your *bathada*,
> You shall be soaked, and stroked, and tubbed, and rubbed:
> And scrubbed, and fubbed, dear Don, before you go.
> You shall, in faith, my scurvy baboon Don:
> Be curried, clawed, and flawed, and tawed, indeed.   100
> I will the heartilier go about it now,
> And make the widow a punk, so much the sooner,
> To be revenged on this impetuous Face:
> The quickly doing of it is the grace.
>
>   [*Exeunt* SUBTLE, SURLY]

Act IV, Scene iv

[*Enter*] FACE, KASTRIL, DAME PLIANT

FACE
> Come lady: I knew, the Doctor would not leave,
> Till he had found the very nick of her fortune.

87 *Hands* Your hand on it
91 By this honoured beard; I fear, sirs, you are practising treachery
     upon me
98 *fubbed* (fobbed) cheated, deceived
100 *flawed* flayed; *tawed* suppled, as leather is when dressed with
     alum
  2 *nick* critical moment, turning point

KASTRIL
  To be a countess, say you?
FACE   A Spanish countess, sir.
PLIANT
  Why? Is that better than an English countess?
FACE
  Better? 'Slight, make you that a question, lady?   5
KASTRIL
  Nay, she is a fool, Captain, you must pardon her.
FACE
  Ask from your courtier, to your Inns of Court-man,
  To your mere milliner: they will tell you all,
  Your Spanish jennet is the best horse. Your Spanish
  Stoop is the best garb. Your Spanish beard   10
  Is the best cut. Your Spanish ruffs are the best
  Wear. Your Spanish pavan the best dance.
  Your Spanish titillation in a glove
  The best perfume. And, for your Spanish pike,
  And Spanish blade, let your poor Captain speak.   15
  Here comes the Doctor.

                [*Enter* SUBTLE]

SUBTLE   My most honoured lady,
  (For so I am now to style you, having found
  By this my scheme, you are to undergo
  An honourable fortune, very shortly.)
  What will you say now, if some—
FACE   I ha' told her all, sir.   20
  And her right worshipful brother, here, that she shall be
  A countess: do not delay 'em, sir. A Spanish countess.
SUBTLE
  Still, my scarce worshipful Captain, you can keep
  No secret. Well, since he has told you, madame,
  Do you forgive him, and I do.
KASTRIL   She shall do that, sir.   25
  I'll look to't, 'tis my charge.
SUBTLE   Well then. Nought rests
  But that she fit her love, now, to her fortune.

10 *Stoop* bow; *garb* fashion   12 *pavan* a grave, stately dance
13 *Spanish titillation* a long, elaborate process of perfuming material
18 *scheme* some horoscope or figure
26 *rests* remains

9–15 *Your Spanish jennet* &c. In the reign of James I Spanish fashions
  were popular at Court, since James wished for closer relations between
  England and Spain, though the people did not.

PLIANT
　Truly, I shall never brook a Spaniard.
SUBTLE　　　　　　　　　　　　　　　No?
PLIANT
　Never, sin' eighty-eight could I abide 'em,
　And that was some three year afore I was born, in truth.　　30
SUBTLE
　Come, you must love him, or be miserable:
　Choose, which you will.
FACE　　　　　　　　　　By this good rush, persuade her,
　She will cry strawberries else, within this twelvemonth.
SUBTLE
　Nay, shads, and mackerel, which is worse.
FACE　　　　　　　　　　　　　　　Indeed, sir?
KASTRIL
　God's lid, you shall love him, or I'll kick you.
PLIANT　　　　　　　　　　　　　　　Why?　　35
　I'll do as you will ha' me, brother.
KASTRIL　　　　　　　　　　Do,
　Or by this hand, I'll maul you.
FACE　　　　　　　　　　Nay, good sir,
　Be not so fierce.
SUBTLE　　　　　　No, my enraged child,
　She will be ruled. What, when she come to taste
　The pleasures of a countess! To be courted—　　40
FACE
　And kissed, and ruffled!
SUBTLE　　　　　　　　　Ay, behind the hangings.
FACE
　And then come forth in pomp!
SUBTLE　　　　　　　　　　And know her state!
FACE
　Of keeping all th'idolators o' the chamber
　Barer to her, than at their prayers!
SUBTLE　　　　　　　　　　　Is served
　Upon the knee!
FACE　　　　　　And has her pages, ushers,　　45
　Footmen, and coaches—

32 *rush* picked up from the floor, which was strewed with rushes
33 *cry strawberries* sink to the position of a market girl
34 *shads* a kind of herring—sinking from market girl to fishwife
41 *ruffled* touzled

29 *Never, sin' eighty-eight.* 1588, the year of the Armada; the allusion is a
common one in seventeenth century poetry.

SUBTLE   Her six mares—
FACE   Nay, eight!
SUBTLE
  To hurry her through London, to th' Exchange,
  Bedlam, the China-houses—
FACE   Yes, and have
  The citizens gape at her, and praise her tires!
  And my lord's goose-turd bands, that rides with her!   50
KASTRIL
  Most brave! By this hand, you are not my suster,
  If you refuse.
PLIANT   I will not refuse, brother.

             [*Enter* SURLY]

SURLY
  Qué es esto, Señores, que no se venga?
  Esta tradanza me mata!
FACE   It is the Count come!
  The Doctor knew he would be here, by his art.   55
SUBTLE
  En galanta madama, Don! Galantissima!
SURLY
  Por todos los dioses, la más acabada
  Hermosura, que he visto en my vida!
FACE
  Is't not a gallant language, that they speak?
KASTRIL
  An admirable language! Is't not French?   60
FACE
  No, Spanish, sir.
KASTRIL   It goes like law-French,
  And that, they say, is the courtliest language.
FACE   List, sir.

49 *tires* attires
50 *goose-turd* yellowish-green
53–4 How is it, gentlemen, that she does not come? This delay is
    killing me.
57–8 By all the gods, the most perfect beauty I have seen in my life.

47–8 *th'Exchange, Bedlam, the China-houses.* Centres of fashionable resort.
  The New Exchange in the Strand, known as 'Britain's Burse', was
  built in 1608–9; Bethlehem Hospital was a place where one could watch
  the madmen for amusement; the China-houses were private houses
  where porcelain, ivory, silks etc. were on view, and, since trade with
  the East had not long been opened, were objects of general interest
  and curiosity.

SURLY
El sol ha perdido su lumbre, con el
Resplandor, que trae esta dama. Válgame Dios!
FACE
He admires your sister.
KASTRIL   Must she not make curtsey?   65
SUBTLE
'Ods will, she must go to him, man; and kiss him!
It is the Spanish fashion, for the women
To make first court.
FACE   'Tis true he tells you, sir:
His art knows all.
SURLY   *Porqué no se acude?*
KASTRIL
He speaks to her, I think?
FACE   That he does sir.   70
SURLY
Por el amor de Dios, qué es esto, que se tarda?
KASTRIL
Nay, see: she will not understand him! Gull.
Noddy.
PLIANT What say you brother?
KASTRIL   Ass, my suster,
Go kuss him, as the cunning man would ha' you,
I'll thrust a pin i' your buttocks else.
FACE   O, no sir.   75
SURLY
Señora mía, mi persona muy indigna está
Á llegar á tanta hermosura.
FACE
Does he not use her bravely?
KASTRIL   Bravely, i' faith!
FACE
Nay, he will use her better.
KASTRIL   Do you think so?
SURLY
Señora, si sera servida, entremos.   80
                    [*Exeunt* SURLY, DAME PLIANT]

63–4 The sun has lost his light with the splendour this lady brings,
    so help me God
69 Why doesn't she come to me?
71 For the love of God, why does she delay?
76–7 My lady, my person is quite unworthy to come near such
    beauty
80 Lady, if it is convenient, we will go in

KASTRIL

Where does he carry her?

FACE   Into the garden, sir;

Take you no thought: I must interpret for her.

SUBTLE

Give Dol the word [*Exit* FACE] Come, my fierce child,
advance,

We'll to our quarrelling lesson again.

KASTRIL   Agreed.

I love a Spanish boy, with all my heart.   85

SUBTLE

Nay, and by this means, sir, you shall be brother

To a great count.

KASTRIL   Ay, I knew that, at first.

This match will advance the house of the Kastrils.

SUBTLE

Pray God, your sister prove but pliant.

KASTRIL   Why,

Her name is so: by her other husband.

SUBTLE   How!   90

KASTRIL

The widow Pliant. Knew you not that?

SUBTLE   No faith, sir.

Yet, by erection of her figure, I guessed it.

Come, let's go practice.

KASTRIL   Yes, but do you think, Doctor,

I e'er shall quarrel well?

SUBTLE   I warrant you.

[*Exeunt* SUBTLE, KASTRIL]

Act IV, Scene v

[*Enter*] DOL, MAMMON

DOL

For, after Alexander's death—   *In her fit of talking*

MAMMON   Good lady—

DOL

That Perdiccas, and Antigonus were slain,

The two that stood, Seleuc', and Ptolomee—

MAMMON

Madam.

83 *the word* i.e. to begin raving
92 *erection of her figure* casting her horoscope

DOL   Made up the two legs, and the fourth Beast.
  That was Gog-north, and Egypt-south: which after   5
  Was called Gog-iron-leg, and South-iron-leg—
MAMMON   Lady—
DOL
  And then Gog-horned. So was Egypt, too.
  Then Egypt-clay-leg, and Gog-clay-leg—
MAMMON   Sweet madam.
DOL
  And last Gog-dust, and Egypt-dust, which fall
  In the last link of the fourth chain. And these   10
  Be stars in story, which none see, or look at—
MAMMON
  What shall I do?
DOL   For, as he says, except
  We call the Rabbins, and the heathen Greeks—
MAMMON
  Dear lady.
DOL   To come from Salem, and from Athens,
  And teach the people of Great Britain—
                    [*Enter* FACE]
FACE   What's the matter, sir?   15
DOL
  To speak the tongue of Eber, and Javan—
MAMMON   O,
  She's in her fit.
DOL   We shall know nothing—
FACE   Death, sir,
  We are undone.
DOL   Where, then, a learned linguist
  Shall see the ancient used communion
  Of vowels, and consonants—
FACE   My master will hear!   20

1–32 *For, after Alexander's death* &c. Dol's raving is made up of scraps
  and fragments quoted from Hugh Broughton's *A Concent of Scripture*
  (1590), an attempt to settle Biblical chronology. Broughton (1549–
  1612) was a theologian and rabbinical scholar, and he was a staunch
  Puritan. Jonson satirises him again in *Volpone*, II.ii, 119. It would be
  pedantry to explain every allusion which Dol makes in her 'fit of
  talking', but Togarmah (27) refers to *Ezekiel*, xxxviii, 6, the description
  of the 'habergeons' as 'Brimstony' comes from Wyclif's version of
  Revelation, xi,17, 'Abaddon, and the Beast of Cittim' are from Broughton's *A Revelation of the Holy Apocalyps* (1610), and refer to the Pope.
  David Kimchi, or Kimhi, was one of a family group of Jewish gram-
  marians and Biblical scholars who worked at Narbonne in the twelfth
  century, Onkelos was a first century scholar and translator, and Abra-
  ham ben Meir Ibn Ezra (1092–1157) a Biblical critic and poet.

DOL
A wisdom, which Pythagoras held most high—
MAMMON
Sweet honourable lady.
DOL   To comprise
All sounds of voices, in few marks of letters—
FACE
Nay, you must never hope to lay her now.

They speak together

DOL	FACE
And so we may arrive by	How did you put her into't?
Talmud skill,	MAMMON Alas I talked 25
And profane Greek, to	Of a fifth monarchy I
raise the building up	would erect,
Of Heber's house, against	With the philosopher's
the Ismaelite,	stone (by chance) and she
King of Togarmah, and his	Falls on the other four,
habergeons	straight. FACE Out of
Brimstony, blue, and fiery;	Broughton!
and the force	I told you so. 'Slid stop
Of King Abaddon, and the	her mouth. MAMMON Is't
Beast of Cittim:	best?
Which Rabbi David	FACE
Kimchi, Onkelos,	She'll never leave else.
And Aben-Ezra do	If the old man hear her, 30
interpret Rome.	We are but fæces, ashes.
	SUBTLE [*within*] What's to do
	there?
	FACE
	O, we are lost. Now she
	hears him, she is quiet.

Upon SUBTLE'S *entry they disperse*

MAMMON
Where shall I hide me?
SUBTLE   How! What sight is here!
Close deeds of darkness, and that shun the light!
Bring him again. Who is he? What, my son!   35
O, I have lived too long.

28 *habergeons* sleeveless coats of mail (used here only for sound)
31 *fæces* dead matter

25 *a fifth monarchy*. The Fifth Monarchy Men were a millenarian sect in
England during the seventeenth century.

MAMMON   Nay good, dear Father,
There was no unchaste purpose.
SUBTLE   Not? And flee me,
When I come in?
MAMMON   That was my error.
SUBTLE   Error?
Guilt, guilt, my son. Give it the right name. No marvel,
If I found check in our great work within,   40
When such affairs as these were managing!
MAMMON
Why, have you so?
SUBTLE   It has stood still this half hour:
And all the rest of our less works gone back.
Where is the instrument of wickedness,
My lewd false drudge?
MAMMON   Nay, good sir, blame not him.   45
Believe me, 'twas against his will, or knowledge.
I saw her by chance.
SUBTLE   Will you commit more sin,
T'excuse a varlet?
MAMMON   By my hope, 'tis true, sir.
SUBTLE
Nay, then I wonder less, if you, for whom
The blessing was prepared, would so tempt heaven: 50
And lose your fortunes.
MAMMON   Why, sir?
SUBTLE   This'll retard
The work, a month at least.
MAMMON   Why, if it do,
What remedy? But think it not, good Father:
Our purposes were honest.
SUBTLE   As they were,
So the reward will prove. How now! Ay me.   55
                    A great crack and noise within
God, and all saints be good to us. What's that?

                    [*Enter* FACE]

FACE
O sir, we are defeated! All the works
Are flown *in fumo*: every glass is burst.

41 *managing* going on
47 *more sin* i.e. perjure yourself
58 *in fumo* in smoke

_____

55 s.d. *A great crack*. All the earlier instructions about 'luting' and her-
    metically sealing the vessels seem like a preparation for this dramatically
    apt explosion.

Furnace, and all rent down! As if a bolt
Of thunder had been driven through the house.   60
Retorts, receivers, pelicans, boltheads,
All struck in shivers! Help, good sir! Alas,

SUBTLE *falls down as in a swoon*

Coldness, and death invades him. Nay, sir Mammon,
Do the fair offices of a man! You stand,
As you were readier to depart, than he.   65
Who's there? My lord her brother is come.

One knocks

MAMMON   Ha, Lungs?
FACE

His coach is at the door. Avoid his sight,
For he's as furious, as his sister is mad.
MAMMON

Alas!
FACE   My brain is quite undone with the fume, sir,
I ne'er must hope to be mine own man again.   70
MAMMON

Is all lost, Lungs? Will nothing be preserved,
Of all our cost?
FACE   Faith, very little, sir.
A peck of coals, or so, which is cold comfort, sir.
MAMMON

O my voluptuous mind! I am justly punished.
FACE

And so am I, sir.
MAMMON   Cast from all my hopes—   75
FACE

Nay, certainties, sir.
MAMMON   By mine own base affections.
SUBTLE

O, the curst fruits of vice, and lust!

SUBTLE *seems to come to himself*

MAMMON   Good father,
It was my sin. Forgive it.
SUBTLE   Hangs my roof
Over us still, and will not fall, O justice,
Upon us, for this wicked man!
FACE   Nay, look, sir,   80
You grieve him, now, with staying in his sight:

62 *shivers* pieces
64 *fair* appropriate, kind
70 *mine own man* myself

    Good sir, the nobleman will come too, and take you,
    And that may breed a tragedy.
MAMMON   I'll go.
FACE
    Ay, and repent at home, sir. It may be,
    For some good penance, you may ha' it, yet,   85
    A hundred pound to the box at Bedlam—
MAMMON   Yes.
FACE
    For the restoring such as ha' their wits.
MAMMON   I'll do't.
FACE
    I'll send one to you to receive it.
MAMMON   Do.
    Is no projection left?
FACE   All flown, or stinks, sir.
MAMMON
    Will nought be saved, that's good for medicine, thinkst thou? 90
FACE
    I cannot tell, sir. There will be, perhaps,
    Something, about the scraping of the shards,
    Will cure the itch: though not your itch of mind, sir.
    It shall be saved for you, and sent home. Good sir,
    This way: for fear the lord should meet you.
                    [*Exit* MAMMON]
SUBTLE   Face.   95
FACE
    Ay.
SUBTLE Is he gone?
FACE   Yes, and as heavily
    As all the gold he hoped for, were in his blood.
    Let us be light, though.
SUBTLE   Ay, as balls, and bound
    And hit our heads against the roof for joy:
    There's so much of our care now cast away.   100
FACE
    Now to our Don.
SUBTLE   Yes, your young widow, by this time
    Is made a countess, Face: she's been in travail
    Of a young heir for you.
FACE   Good, sir.
SUBTLE   Off with your case,

---

86 *Bedlam* Bethlehem hospital for the insane
92 *shards* pots
103 *case* his uniform as Lungs; to Dame Pliant he is Captain Face

And greet her kindly, as a bridegroom should,
After these common hazards.
FACE   Very well, sir.   105
Will you go fetch Don Diego off, the while?
SUBTLE
And fetch him over too, if you'll be pleased, sir:
Would Dol were in her place, to pick his pockets now.
FACE
Why, you can do it as well, if you would set to't.
I pray you prove your virtue.
SUBTLE   For your sake, sir.   110

                    [*Exeunt* SUBTLE *and* FACE]

Act IV, Scene vi

[*Enter*] SURLY, DAME PLIANT

SURLY
Lady, you see into what hands, you are fallen;
'Mongst what a nest of villains! And how near
Your honour was t'have catched a certain clap
(Through your credulity) had I but been
So punctually forward, as place, time,   5
And other circumstance would ha' made a man:
For you're a handsome woman: would you're wise, too.
I am a gentleman, come here disguised,
Only to find the knaveries of this citadel,
And where I might have wronged your honour, and have not, 10
I claim some interest in your love. You are,
They say, a widow, rich: and I am a bachelor,
Worth nought: your fortunes may make me a man,
As mine ha' preserved you a woman. Think upon it,
And whether, I have deserved you, or no.
PLIANT   I will, sir.   15
SURLY
And for these household-rogues, let me alone,
To treat with them.

[*Enter* SUBTLE]

SUBTLE   How doth my noble Diego?
And my dear madam, Countess? Hath the Count

107 *fetch him over* get the better of him
110 *prove your virtue* test your skill
  5 *punctually forward* ready to take advantage
  9 *Only* solely

Been courteous, lady? Liberal? And open?
Donzell, me thinks you look melancholic,   20
After your *coitum*, and scurvy! Truly,
I do not like the dulness of your eye:
It hath a heavy cast, 'tis upsee Dutch,
And says you are a lumpish whore-master.
Be lighter, I will make your pockets so.   25
                 He falls to picking of them
SURLY
Will you, Don bawd, and pickpurse? How now? Reel you?
Stand up sir, you shall find since I am so heavy,
I'll gi' you equal weight.
SUBTLE   Help, murder!
SURLY   No, sir.
There's no such thing intended. A good cart,
And a clean whip shall ease you of that fear.   30
I am the Spanish Don, that should be cozened,
Do you see? Cozened? Where's your Captain Face?
That parcel-broker, and whole-bawd, all rascal.

                 [*Enter* FACE]

FACE
How, Surly!
SURLY   O, make your approach, good Captain.
I have found, from whence your copper rings, and spoons   35
Come now, wherewith you cheat abroad in taverns.
'Twas here, you learned t'anoint your boot with brimstone,
Then rub men's gold on't, for a kind of touch,
And say 'twas naught, when you had changed the colour,
That you might ha't for nothing? And this Doctor,   40
Your sooty, smoky-bearded compeer, he
Will close you so much gold, in a bolt's head,
And, on a turn, convey (i' the stead) another
With sublimed mercury, that shall burst i' the heat,
And fly out all *in fumo*? Then weeps Mammon: 45

19 *courteous, Liberal, open* with sexual overtones, applied to the lady
23 *upsee Dutch* Dutch fashion, phlegmatic
41 *compeer* companion
43 *on a turn* i.e. by sleight of hand

---

21 *After your coitum.* Omne animal post coitum triste est. See *John Donne: The Elegies and The Songs and Sonnets*, ed. Gardner (Oxford 1956), p. 213.
33 *parcel-broker.* Part-time go-between. 'Broker' usually meant pawn-broker, but always referred to an agent, middleman, factor, and was a term of abuse. Cf. *Everyman in His Humour*, III.v, 32, 'One of the deuil's neere kinsmen, a broker'.

Then swoons his worship. Or, he is the Faustus,

[FACE *slips out*]

That casteth figures, and can conjure, cures
Plague, piles, and pox, by the ephemerides,
And holds intelligence with all the bawds,
And midwives of three shires? While you send in—   50
Captain, (what is he gone?) damsels with child,
Wives, that are barren, or, the waiting-maid
With the green sickness? [SUBTLE *attempts to leave*] Nay,

sir, you must tarry

Though he be 'scaped; and answer, by the ears, sir.

Act IV, Scene vii

[*Enter*] FACE, KASTRIL, SURLY, SUBTLE

FACE

Why, now's the time, if ever you will quarrel
Well (as they say) and be a true-born child.
The Doctor, and your sister both are abused.

KASTRIL

Where is he? Which is he? He is a slave
Whate'er he is, and the son of a whore. Are you   5
The man, sir, I would know?

SURLY   I should be loath, sir,

To confess so much.

KASTRIL   Then you lie, i' your throat.

SURLY   How?

FACE

A very errant rogue, sir, and a cheater,
Employed here, by another conjurer,
That does not love the Doctor, and would cross him   10
If he knew how—

SURLY   Sir, you are abused.

KASTRIL   You lie:

And 'tis no matter.

FACE   Well said, sir. He is

The impudentest rascal—

SURLY   You are indeed. Will you hear me, sir?

FACE

By no means: bid him be gone.

46 *Faustus* familiar from Marlowe's play
47 *figures* horoscopes
48 *ephemerides* astronomical almanacs
53 *green sickness* chlorosis, a form of anaemia
54 *by the ears* in the pillory

KASTRIL   Be gone, sir, quickly.

SURLY

This's strange! Lady, do you inform your brother.   15

FACE

There is not such a foist, in all the town,
The Doctor had him, presently: and finds, yet,
The Spanish Count will come, here. Bear up, Subtle.

SUBTLE

Yes, sir, he must appear, within this hour.

FACE

And yet this rogue, would come, in a disguise,   20
By the temptation of another spirit,
To trouble our art, though he could not hurt it.

KASTRIL   Ay,
I know—away, you talk like a foolish mauther.

SURLY

Sir, all is truth, she says.

FACE   Do not believe him, sir:
He is the lyingest swabber! Come your ways, sir.   25

SURLY

You are valiant, out of company.

KASTRIL   Yes, how then, sir?

[Enter DRUGGER]

Nay, here's an honest fellow too, that knows him,
And all his tricks. (Make good what I say, Abel,)
This cheater would ha' cozened thee o' the widow.
He owes this honest Drugger, here, seven pound,   30
He has had on him, in two-penny 'orths of tobacco.

DRUGGER

Yes sir. And he's damned himself, three terms, to pay me.

FACE

And what does he owe for *lotium*?

DRUGGER   Thirty shillings, sir:
And for six syringes.

SURLY   ,   Hydra of villany!

16 *foist* pickpocket, rogue
21 i.e. set on by another conjurer
23 *mauther* a great awkward girl
31 *on* from
33 *lotium* stale urine used by barbers as a 'lye' for the hair

34 *Hydra*. The seventh labour of Hercules was to kill the Hydra, the
many-headed snake of the marsh of Lerna; its heads grew again twice
as fast as he cut them off. Surly, here, sees himself losing through the
multiplication of his enemies.

FACE
  Nay, sir, you must quarrel him out o' the house.
KASTRIL   I will.   35
  Sir, if you get not out o' doors, you lie:
  And you are a pimp.
SURLY   Why, this is madness, sir,
  Not valour in you: I must laugh at this.
KASTRIL
  It is my humour: you are a pimp, and a trig,
  And an Amadis de Gaul, or a Don Quixote.   40
DRUGGER
  Or a knight o' the curious coxcomb. Do you see?

                    [*Enter* ANANIAS]

ANANIAS
  Peace to the household.
KASTRIL   I'll keep peace, for no man.
ANANIAS
  Casting of dollars is concluded lawful.
KASTRIL
  Is he the constable?
SUBTLE   Peace, Ananias.
FACE   No, sir.
KASTRIL
  Then you are an otter, and a shad, a whit,   45
  A very tim.
SURLY   You'll hear me, sir?
KASTRIL   I will not.
ANANIAS
  What is the motive!
SURLY   Zeal, in the young gentleman,
  Against his Spanish slops—
ANANIAS   They are profane,
  Lewd, superstitious, and idolatrous breeches.

  39 *trig* dandy, coxcomb
  45 *whit* bawd (*cf.* Captain Whit in *Bartholomew Fair*)
  46 *tim* meaning unknown

  ---

  39 *It is my humour.* See *Every Man Out of his Humour*, Induction, 110–14.
  40 *an Amadis de Gaul* &c. a Spanish or Portuguese romance, written in the
     form in which we have it by Garcia de Montalvo *circa* 1450–1500. It was
     early translated into French, and many continuations were written,
     relating to the son and nephew of Amadis. 'The introduction of his
     name here, coupled with that of the hero of the greatest satire on chivalry,
     fitly keeps up the bizarre nature of Kastril's conversation' (Hathaway).
     See Edwin B. Knowles, 'Allusions to "Don Quixote" before 1660',
     Philological Quarterly, XX, 4 (October 1941) 573–86.

SURLY
  New rascals!
KASTRIL   Will you be gone, sir?
ANANIAS   Avoid Satan,   50
  Thou art not of the light. That ruff of pride,
  About thy neck, betrays thee: and is the same
  With that, which the unclean birds, in seventy-seven,
  Were seen to prank it with, on divers coasts.
  Thou lookest like Antichrist, in that lewd hat.   55
SURLY
  I must give way.
KASTRIL   Be gone, sir.
SURLY   But I'll take
  A course with you—
(ANANIAS   Depart, proud Spanish fiend)
SURLY
  Captain, and Doctor—
ANANIAS   Child of perdition.
KASTRIL   Hence, sir.
                              [*Exit* SURLY]
  Did I not quarrel bravely?
FACE   Yes, indeed, sir.
KASTRIL
  Nay, and I give my mind to't, I shall do't.   60
FACE
  O, you must follow, sir, and threaten him tame.
  He'll turn again else.
KASTRIL   I'll re-turn him, then.
                              [*Exit* KASTRIL]
FACE
  Drugger, this rogue prevented us, for thee:
  We had determined, that thou shouldst ha' come,
  In a Spanish suit, and ha' carried her so; and he   65
  A brokerly slave, goes, puts it on himself.

53 *unclean birds* allusion to *Revelation* xviii,2: *cf.* V.iii, 47
56–7 *take a course* be revenged   60 *and* if
63 *prevented us, for thee* anticipated what we intended for you
64 *determined* decided   65 *carried* won
66 *brokerly* pettifogging

53 *the unclean birds, in seventy-seven.* This allusion has never been fully
  explained. Herford and Simpson suggest that the date is an error, and
  should read either 'sixty-seven' (the date of D'Alva's invasion of the
  Netherlands) or 'eighty-eight' (the year of the Armada). More con-
  vincing is Hathaway's conjecture that they are birds in some popular
  superstition, the details of which have not survived. The context
  supports the impression of a contemporary joke.

Hast brought the damask?
DRUGGER   Yes sir.
FACE   Thou must borrow,
  A Spanish suit. Hast thou no credit with the players?
DRUGGER
  Yes, sir, did you never see me play the fool?
FACE
  I know not, Nab: thou shalt, if I can help it.   70
  Hieronymo's old cloak, ruff, and hat will serve,
  I'll tell thee more, when thou bring'st 'em.
                                        [*Exit* DRUGGER]
ANANIAS   Sir, I know
  SUBTLE *hath whispered with him this while*
  The Spaniard hates the Brethren, and hath spies
  Upon their actions: and that this was one
  I make no scruple. But the holy Synod   75
  Have been in prayer, and meditation, for it.
  And 'tis revealed no less, to them, than me,
  That casting of money is most lawful.
SUBTLE   True.
  But here, I cannot do it; if the house
  Should chance to be suspected, all would out,   80
  And we be locked up, in the Tower, forever,
  To make gold there (for th' state) never come out:
  And, then, are you defeated.
ANANIAS   I will tell
  This to the Elders, and the weaker Brethren,
  That the whole company of the Separation   85
  May join in humble prayer again.
(SUBTLE   And fasting.)
ANANIAS
  Yea, for some fitter place. The peace of mind
  Rest with these walls.
SUBTLE   Thanks, courteous Ananias.
                                    [*Exit* ANANIAS]

FACE
  What did he come for?
SUBTLE   About casting dollars,
  Presently, out of hand. And so, I told him,   90
  A Spanish minister came here to spy,
  Against the faithful—
FACE   I conceive. Come Subtle,

70 *help* forward
71 *Hieronymo* hero of Kyd's *Spanish Tragedy*
75 *scruple* doubt   90 *Presently* now, at once

Thou art so down upon the least disaster!
How wouldst th' ha' done, if I had not helped thee out?
SUBTLE
I thank thee Face, for the angry boy, i' faith.   95
FACE
Who would ha' looked, it should ha' been that rascal?
Surly? He had dyed his beard, and all. Well, sir,
Here's damask come, to make you a suit.
SUBTLE   Where's Drugger?
FACE
He is gone to borrow me a Spanish habit,
I'll be the Count, now.
SUBTLE   But where's the widow?   100
FACE
Within, with my lord's sister: Madam Dol
Is entertaining her.
SUBTLE   By your favour, Face,
Now she is honest, I will stand again.
FACE
You will not offer it?
SUBTLE   Why?
FACE   Stand to your word,
Or—here comes Dol. She knows—
SUBTLE   You're tyrannous still.   105

[*Enter* DOL]

FACE
Strict for my right. How now, Dol? Hast told her,
The Spanish Count will come?
DOL   Yes, but another is come,
You little looked for!
FACE   Who's that?
DOL   Your master:
The master of the house.
SUBTLE   How, Dol!
FACE   She lies.
This is some trick. Come, leave your quiblins, Dorothy.   110
DOL
Look out, and see.
SUBTLE   Art thou in earnest?
DOL   'Slight,
Forty o' the neighbours are about him, talking.

 93 *down* dejected   96 *looked* foreseen
103 *stand* make a bid for her   105 *still* always
110 *quiblins* tricks

FACE

  'Tis he, by this good day.

DOL   'Twill prove ill day,

  For some on us.

FACE   We are undone, and taken.

DOL

  Lost, I am afraid.

SUBTLE   You said he would not come,   115

  While there died one a week, within the liberties.

FACE

  No: 'twas within the walls.

SUBTLE   Was't so? Cry you mercy:

  I thought the liberties. What shall we do now, Face?

FACE

  Be silent: not a word, if he call, or knock.

  I'll into mine old shape again, and meet him,   120

  Of Jeremy, the butler. I' the mean time,

  Do you two pack up all the goods, and purchase,

  That we can carry i' the two trunks. I'll keep him

  Off for today, if I cannot longer: and then

  At night, I'll ship you both away to Ratcliff,   125

  Where we'll meet tomorrow, and there we'll share.

  Let Mammon's brass, and pewter keep the cellar:

  We'll have another time for that. But, Dol,

  Pray thee, go heat a little water, quickly,

  Subtle must shave me. All my Captain's beard   130

  Must off, to make me appear smooth Jeremy.

  You'll do't?

SUBTLE   Yes, I'll shave you, as well as I can.

FACE

  And not cut my throat, but trim me?

SUBTLE   You shall see, sir.

                          [*Exeunt* SUBTLE, FACE, DOL]

116 *liberties* suburbs
117 see I.i, 182
122 *purchase* winnings

---

125 *Ratcliff.* In Stepney. It was an important place of resort at the time, because of the highway of the river.

Act V, Scene i

[Enter] LOVEWIT, NEIGHBOURS

LOVEWIT
  Has there been such resort, say you?

NEIGHBOUR 1   Daily, sir.

NEIGHBOUR 2
  And nightly, too.

NEIGHBOUR 3   Ay, some as brave as lords.

NEIGHBOUR 4
  Ladies, and gentlewomen.

NEIGHBOUR 5   Citizens' wives.

NEIGHBOUR 1
  And knights.

NEIGHBOUR 6   In coaches.

NEIGHBOUR 2   Yes, and oyster-women.

NEIGHBOUR 1
  Beside other gallants.

NEIGHBOUR 3   Sailors' wives.

NEIGHBOUR 4   Tobacco-men.   5

NEIGHBOUR 5
  Another Pimlico!

LOVEWIT   What should my knave advance,
  To draw this company? He hung out no banners
  Of a strange calf, with five legs, to be seen?
  Or a huge lobster, with six claws?

NEIGHBOUR 6   No, sir.

NEIGHBOUR 3
  We had gone in then, sir.

LOVEWIT   He has no gift   10
  Of teaching i' the nose, that e'er I knew of!
  You saw no bills set up, that promised cure
  Of agues, or the toothache?

---

6 *advance* set forth, advertise
11 *teaching i' the nose* i.e. preaching like a Puritan

---

6 *Pimlico*. Not the district, but a house noted for cakes and 'Pimlico' ale at Hoxton. It is described in *Pimlico, Or Runne Red-Cap. Tis a mad world at Hogsdon*, 1609.

8 *a strange calf, with five legs*. See *Bartholomew Fair*, III.vi, 7, and V.iv, 84–5.

12–13 *cure of agues, or the toothache*. The idea of a fairground still plays behind Lovewit's questions. Mountebanks and itinerant tooth-drawers were part of every fair. For the latter see Chettle, *Kind-Harts Dreame*, 1592 (*Bodley Head Quartos*, IV, 1923, 31–4).

NEIGHBOUR 2   No such thing, sir.

LOVEWIT
  Nor heard a drum struck, for baboons, or puppets?

NEIGHBOUR 5
  Neither, sir.

LOVEWIT   What device should he bring forth now!   15
  I love a teeming wit, as I love my nourishment.
  Pray God he ha' not kept such open house,
  That he hath sold my hangings, and my bedding:
  I left him nothing else. If he have eat 'em,
  A plague o' the moth, say I. Sure he has got   20
  Some bawdy pictures, to call all this ging;
  The friar, and the nun; or the new motion
  Of the knight's courser, covering the parson's mare;
  The boy of six year old, with the great thing:
  Or 't may be, he has the fleas that run at tilt,   25
  Upon a table, or some dog to dance?
  When saw you him?

NEIGHBOUR 1   Who sir, Jeremy?

NEIGHBOUR 2   Jeremy butler?
  We saw him not this month.

LOVEWIT   How!

NEIGHBOUR 4   Not these five weeks, sir.

NEIGHBOUR 1
  These six weeks, at the least.

LOVEWIT   Y' amaze me, neighbours!

NEIGHBOUR 5
  Sure, if your worship know not where he is,   30
  He's slipped away.

NEIGHBOUR 6   Pray God, he be not made away!

LOVEWIT
  Ha? It's no time to question, then.   *He knocks*

---

14 *baboons, or puppets* popular entertainments
15 *device* ingenious invention   21 *ging* company, gang
25 *run at tilt* joust   31 *made away* murdered

---

14 *puppets.* Herford and Simpson quote several instances in support of
their statement that Jonson held puppets in contempt. This is true, but
it should be noted that he uses them for brilliant satiric effects in the
fifth act of *Bartholomew Fair.*

22–5 *The friar, and the nun* &c. These curiosities appear to have been
actually exhibited in London at the time. See T. Heywood, *If You
know not me*, part ii, 1606, sig. D3 ('her's the Fryer whipping the
Nuns arse'); Beaumont and Fletcher, *The Knight of the Burning Pestle*,
III.i ('the little child that was so faire growne about the members');
The Devil is an Ass, V.ii, 10–13 ('I would sooner Keepe fleas within a
circle').

NEIGHBOUR 6   About
  Some three weeks since, I heard a doleful cry,
  As I sat up, a-mending my wife's stockings.
LOVEWIT
  This's strange! That none will answer! Didst thou hear   35
  A cry, saist thou?
NEIGHBOUR 6   Yes, sir, like unto a man
  That had been strangled an hour, and could not speak.
NEIGHBOUR 2
  I heard it too, just this day three weeks, at two o'clock
  Next morning.
LOVEWIT   These be miracles, or you make 'em so!
  A man an hour strangled, and could not speak,   40
  And both you heard him cry?
NEIGHBOUR 3   Yes, downward, sir.
LOVEWIT
  Thou art a wise fellow: give me thy hand I pray thee.
  What trade art thou on?
NEIGHBOUR 3   A smith, and't please your worship.
LOVEWIT
  A smith? Then, lend me thy help, to get this door open.
NEIGHBOUR 3
  That I will presently, sir, but fetch my tools—
                                   [*Exit* NEIGHBOUR 3]
NEIGHBOUR 1   45
  Sir, best to knock again, afore you break it.

Act V, Scene ii

LOVEWIT
  I will.

                         [*Enter* FACE]

FACE   What mean you, sir?
NEIGHBOURS 1, 2, 4   O, here's Jeremy!
FACE
  Good sir, come from the door.
LOVEWIT   Why! What's the matter?

37 *an hour* not meant literally, though Lovewit takes it so
41 *downward* indeed (probably)

_____

V.ii. Most editors have noted that this scene seems to have been suggested by
  similar trickery in the *Mostellaria* ('Haunted House') of Plautus. There
  is considerable correspondence of incident, and in both plays the intelligence and wit of the cozeners is vindicated in the resolution.

FACE
Yet farther, you are too near, yet.
LOVEWIT   I'the name of wonder!
What means the fellow?
FACE   The house, sir, has been visited.
LOVEWIT
What? With the plague? Stand thou then farther.
FACE   No, sir,   5
I had it not.
LOVEWIT   Who had it then? I left
None else, but thee, i'the house!
FACE   Yes, sir. My fellow,
The cat, that kept the buttery, had it on her
A week, before I spied it: but I got her
Conveyed away, i'the night. And so I shut   10
The house up for a month—
LOVEWIT   How!
FACE   Purposing then, sir,
T'have burnt rose-vinegar, treacle, and tar,
And, ha' made it sweet, that you should ne'er ha' known it:
Because I knew the news would but afflict you, sir.
LOVEWIT
Breathe less, and farther off. Why, this is stranger!   15
The neighbours tell me all, here, that the doors
Have still been open—
FACE   How, sir!
LOVEWIT   Gallants, men, and women,
And of all sorts, tag-rag, been seen to flock here
In threaves, these ten weeks, as to a second Hogsden,
In days of Pimlico, and Eye-bright!
FACE   Sir,   20
Their wisdoms will not say so!
LOVEWIT   Today, they speak

19 *threaves* droves

---

19 *Hogsden*. Now Hoxton, a place much favoured for holidays by the
London citizens.
20 *Eye-bright*. See note to V.i, 6. 'Eye-bright' is quoted in *Pimlico, Or
Runne Red-Cap*, sig. D3ᵛ, and the passage is given by Herford and
Simpson without comment:

> *Eye-bright*, (so fam'd of late for *Beere*)
> Although thy *Name* be numbred heere, – i.e. at Hoxton –
> Thine ancient *Honors* now runne low;
> Thou art struck blind by *Pimlyco*.

O.E.D. suggests that it might be 'A kind of ale in Elizabeth's time', but
from the quotation above it seems more likely to be either the name of
an inn, or the nickname of the innkeeper.

Of coaches, and gallants; one in a French hood,
Went in, they tell me: and another was seen
In a velvet gown, at the window! Divers more
Pass in and out!
FACE   They did pass through the doors then,   25
Or walls, I assure their eyesights, and their spectacles;
For here, sir, are the keys: and here have been,
In this my pocket, now, above twenty days!
And for before, I kept the fort alone, there.
But, that 'tis yet not deep i'the afternoon,   30
I should believe my neighbours had seen double
Through the black pot, and made these apparitions!
For, on my faith, to your worship, for these three weeks,
And upwards, the door has not been opened.
LOVEWIT   Strange!
NEIGHBOUR 1
Good faith, I think I saw a coach!
NEIGHBOUR 2   And I too,   35
I'd ha' been sworn!
LOVEWIT   Do you but think it now?
And but one coach?
NEIGHBOUR 4   We cannot tell, sir: Jeremy
Is a very honest fellow.
FACE   Did you see me at all?
NEIGHBOUR 1
No. That we are sure on.
NEIGHBOUR 2   I'll be sworn o' that.
LOVEWIT
Fine rogues, to have your testimonies built on!   40
              [*Enter* NEIGHBOUR 3 *with his tools*]
NEIGHBOUR 3
Is Jeremy come?
NEIGHBOUR 1   O, yes, you may leave your tools,
We were deceived, he says.
NEIGHBOUR 2   He has had the keys:
And the door has been shut these three weeks.
NEIGHBOUR 3   Like enough.
LOVEWIT
Peace, and get hence, you changelings.

              [*Enter* SURLY *and* MAMMON]

FACE   Surly come!
And Mammon made acquainted? They'll tell all.   45

22 *one in a French hood* Dame Pliant (II.vi, 33)
24 *In a velvet gown* Dol (V.iv, 134)

(How shall I beat them off? What shall I do?)
Nothing's more wretched, than a guilty conscience.

Act V, Scene iii

SURLY
　No, sir, he was a great physician. This,
　It was no bawdy-house: but a mere chancel.
　You knew the lord, and his sister.
MAMMON　　　　　　　　　　　Nay, good Surly—
SURLY
　The happy word, 'be rich'—
MAMMON　　　　　　　　　Play not the tyrant—
SURLY
　Should be today pronounced, to all your friends.　　　5
　And where be your andirons now? And your brass pots?
　That should ha' been golden flagons, and great wedges?
MAMMON
　Let me but breathe. What! They ha' shut their doors,
　Me thinks!　　　　　MAMMON *and* SURLY *knock*
SURLY　　　　Ay, now, 'tis holiday with them.
MAMMON　　　　　　　　　　　　Rogues,
　Cozeners, imposters, bawds.
FACE　　　　　　　　　　What mean you, sir?　　　10
MAMMON
　To enter if we can.
FACE　　　　　　　　Another man's house?
　Here is the owner, sir. Turn you to him,
　And speak your business.
MAMMON　　　　　　　　Are you, sir, the owner?
LOVEWIT
　Yes, sir.
MAMMON　And are those knaves, within, your cheaters?
LOVEWIT
　What knaves? What cheaters?
MAMMON　　　　　　　　　Subtle, and his Lungs.　　　15
FACE
　The gentleman is distracted, sir! No lungs,
　Nor lights ha' been seen here these three weeks, sir,
　Within these doors, upon my word!
SURLY　　　　　　　　　Your word,
　Groom arrogant?
FACE　　　　　Yes, sir, I am the housekeeper,
　And know the keys ha' not been out o' my hands.　　　20

　2 *mere* absolute

SURLY
  This's a new Face?
FACE   You do mistake the house, sir!
  What sign was't at?
SURLY   You rascal! This is one
  O' the confederacy. Come, let's get officers,
  And force the door.
LOVEWIT   Pray you stay, gentlemen.
SURLY
  No, sir, we'll come with warrant.
MAMMON   Ay, and then,   25
  We shall ha' your doors open.
                              [*Exeunt* SURLY, MAMMON]
LOVEWIT   What means this?
FACE
  I cannot tell, sir!
NEIGHBOUR 1   These are two o' the gallants,
  That we do think we saw.
FACE   Two o' the fools?
  You talk as idly as they. Good faith, sir,
  I think the moon has crazed 'em all!

                    [*Enter* KASTRIL]

                              (O me,   30
  The angry boy come too? He'll make a noise,
  And ne'er away till he have betrayed us all.)
KASTRIL
  What rogues, bawds, slaves, you'll open the door anon,
                              KASTRIL *knocks*
  Punk, cockatrice, my suster. By this light
  I'll fetch the marshal to you. You are a whore,   35
  To keep your castle—
FACE   Who would you speak with, sir?
KASTRIL
  The bawdy Doctor, and the cozening Captain,
  And Puss my suster.
LOVEWIT   This is something, sure!
FACE
  Upon my trust, the doors were never open, sir.

  21 *This's a new Face?* i.e. is this yet another trickster?
  22 *sign* as of a tavern   35 *marshal cf.* I.i, 120

  ───

  34 *cockatrice.* A mythical reptile, also called the basilisk, hatched by a
    serpent from a cock's egg, and fabled to kill by its mere glance. Hence,
    it was applied to persons in the sense of monster; and especially to a
    prostitute. Cf. *Poetaster*, IV.vii, 6.

KASTRIL

I have heard all their tricks, told me twice over,   40
By the fat knight, and the lean gentleman.

LOVEWIT

Here comes another.

[*Enter* ANANIAS, TRIBULATION]

FACE   Ananias too?

And his pastor?

TRIBULATION   The doors are shut against us.

ANANIAS

Come forth, you seed of sulphur, sons of fire,
        They beat too, at the door
Your stench, it is broke forth: abomination   45
Is in the house.

KASTRIL   Ay, my suster's there.

ANANIAS   The place,

It is become a cage of unclean birds.

KASTRIL

Yes, I will fetch the scavenger, and the constable.

TRIBULATION

You shall do well.

ANANIAS   We'll join, to weed them out.

KASTRIL

You will not come then? Punk, device, my suster!   50

ANANIAS

Call her not sister. She is a harlot, verily.

KASTRIL

I'll raise the street.

LOVEWIT   Good gentlemen, a word.

ANANIAS

Satan, avoid, and hinder not our zeal.
                [*Exeunt* ANANIAS, TRIBULATION, KASTRIL]

LOVEWIT

The world's turned Bedlam.

FACE   These are all broke loose,

Out of St. Katherine's, where they use to keep,   55
The better sort of mad folks.

NEIGHBOUR 1   All these persons

We saw go in, and out, here.

41 i.e. Mammon and Surly, whose Spanish dress made him appear
    fatter: *cf.* IV.iii, 28
50 *Punk, device* i.e. arrant whore: a play on 'point-device', faultlessly
    exact in dress
55 *St. Katherine's* a hospital founded by Queen Matilda in 1148

NEIGHBOUR 2   Yes, indeed, sir.
NEIGHBOUR 3
  These were the parties.
FACE   Peace, you drunkards. Sir,
  I wonder at it! Please you, to give me leave
  To touch the door, I'll try, and the lock be changed.   60
LOVEWIT
  It mazes me!
FACE   Good faith, sir, I believe,
  There's no such thing. 'Tis all *deceptio visus*.
  (Would I could get him away.)   *Dapper cries out within*
DAPPER   Master Captain, master Doctor.
LOVEWIT
  Who's that?
FACE   (Our clerk within, that I forgot!) I know not, sir.
DAPPER
  For God's sake, when will her Grace be at leisure?
FACE   Ha!   65
  Illusions, some spirit o' the air: (his gag is melted,
  And now he sets out the throat.)
DAPPER   I am almost stifled—
FACE
  (Would you were altogether.)
LOVEWIT   'Tis i' the house.
  Ha! List.
FACE   Believe it, sir, i' the air!
LOVEWIT   Peace, you—
DAPPER
  Mine aunt's Grace does not use me well.
SUBTLE [*within*]   You fool,   70
  Peace, you'll mar all.
FACE   Or you will else, you rogue.
LOVEWIT
  O, is it so? Then you converse with spirits!
  Come sir. No more o' your tricks, good Jeremy,
  The truth, the shortest way.
FACE   Dismiss this rabble, sir.
  What shall I do? I am catched.
LOVEWIT   Good neighbours,   75
  I thank you all. You may depart.   [*Exeunt* NEIGHBOURS]
                    Come sir,
  You know that I am an indulgent master:

62 *deceptio visus* an optical illusion
67 *sets out the throat* raises his voice

And therefore, conceal nothing. What's your medicine,
To draw so many several sorts of wild fowl?

FACE

Sir, you were wont to affect mirth, and wit: 80
(But here's no place to talk on't i' the street.)
Give me but leave, to make the best of my fortune,
And only pardon me th'abuse of your house:
It's all I beg. I'll help you to a widow,
In recompense, that you shall gi' me thanks for,   85
Will make you seven years younger, and a rich one.
'Tis but your putting on a Spanish cloak,
I have her within. You need not fear the house,
It was not visited.

LOVEWIT   But by me, who came
Sooner than you expected.

FACE   It is true, sir.   90
Pray you forgive me.

LOVEWIT   Well: let's see your widow.

[*Exeunt* LOVEWIT, FACE]

Act V, Scene iv

[*Enter* SUBTLE, DAPPER]

SUBTLE

How! Ha' you eaten your gag?

DAPPER   Yes faith, it crumbled
Away i' my mouth.

SUBTLE   You ha' spoiled all then.

DAPPER   No,
I hope my aunt of Fairy will forgive me.

SUBTLE

Your aunt's a gracious lady: but in troth
You were to blame.

DAPPER   The fume did overcome me,   5
And I did do't to stay my stomach. Pray you
So satisfy her Grace. Here comes the Captain.

[*Enter* FACE]

FACE

How now! Is his mouth down?

78 *medicine* charm, spell (see *O.E.D.*)
79 *draw* decoy

---

8 Hathaway notes that at the end of Act IV Face had his beard shaved to
make him appear 'smooth Jeremy', and he has no time to procure a
false one; the pace and economy of these final scenes make such things
unnecessary.

SUBTLE   Ay! He has spoken!

FACE

(A pox, I heard him, and you too.) He's undone, then.
(I have been fain to say, the house is haunted   10
With spirits, to keep churl back.

SUBTLE   And hast thou done it?

FACE

Sure, for this night.

SUBTLE   Why, then triumph, and sing
Of Face so famous, the precious king
Of present wits.

FACE   Did you not hear the coil,
About the door?

SUBTLE   Yes, and I dwindled with it.)   15

FACE

Show him his aunt, and let him be dispatched:
I'll send her to you.   [*Exit* FACE]

SUBTLE   Well sir, your aunt her Grace,
Will give you audience presently, on my suit,
And the Captain's word, that you did not eat your gag,
In any contempt of her Highness.

DAPPER   Not I, in troth, sir.   20

                  [*Enter*] DOL *like the Queen of Fairy*

SUBTLE

Here she is come. Down o' your knees, and wriggle:
She has a stately presence. Good. Yet nearer,
And bid, God save you.

DAPPER   Madam.

SUBTLE   And your aunt.

DAPPER

And my most gracious aunt, God save your Grace.

DOL

Nephew, we thought to have been angry with you: 25
But that sweet face of yours, hath turned the tide,
And made it flow with joy, that ebbed of love.
Arise, and touch our velvet gown.

SUBTLE   The skirts,
And kiss 'em. So.

11 *churl* countryman (because of his hop-yards I.i, 184)
12 *triumph* accented on the second syllable
14 *coil* fuss, disturbance
15 *dwindled* shrank (see quotation in *O.E.D.*)

---

12 *Why, then triumph, and sing* &c. This may perhaps be a quotation from,
or parody of, a popular song.

DOL   Let me now stroke that head,
  Much, nephew, shalt thou win; much shalt thou spend;   30
  Much shalt thou give away: much shalt thou lend.
SUBTLE
  (Ay, much, indeed.) Why do you not thank her Grace?
DAPPER
  I cannot speak, for joy.
SUBTLE   See, the kind wretch!
  Your Grace's kinsman right.
DOL   Give me the bird.
  Here is your fly in a purse, about your neck, cousin,   35
  Wear it, and feed it, about this day se'ennight,
  On your right wrist—
SUBTLE   Open a vein, with a pin,
  And let it suck but once a week: till then,
  You must not look on't.
DOL   No. And, kinsman,
  Bear yourself worthy of the blood you come on.   40
SUBTLE
  Her Grace would ha' you eat no more Woolsack pies,
  Nor Dagger frumety.
DOL   Nor break his fast,
  In Heaven, and Hell.
SUBTLE   She's with you everywhere!
  Nor play with costermongers, at mum-chance, tray-trip,
  God make you rich, (whenas your aunt has done it:)
                                              but keep   45
  The gallantest company, and the best games—
DAPPER   Yes, sir.
SUBTLE
  Gleek and primero: and what you get, be true to us.
DAPPER
  By this hand, I will.
SUBTLE   You may bring's a thousand pound,
  Before tomorrow night, (if but three thousand,
  Be stirring) and you will.

41-2 *Woolsack ... Dagger* famous taverns (see I.i, 191)
42 *frumety* a dish made of hulled wheat boiled in milk, and seasoned
43 *Heaven, and Hell* two taverns on the site of the present committee-
   rooms of the House of Commons (HS)
44 *mum-chance* a dice game;
   tray-trip a dice game that depended on throwing threes
45 *God make you rich* a variety of backgammon

47 *Gleek and primero*. These were the 'best games' because they were the
   games played by the Court.

DAPPER   I swear, I will then.   50
SUBTLE
  Your fly will learn you all games.
FACE [*within*]   Ha' you done there?
SUBTLE
  Your grace will command him no more duties?
DOL   No:
  But come, and see me often. I may chance
  To leave him three or four hundred chests of treasure,
  And some twelve thousand acres of Fairyland: 55
  If he game well, and comely, with good gamesters.
SUBTLE
  There's a kind aunt! Kiss her departing part.
  But you must sell your forty mark a year, now:
DAPPER
  Ay, sir, I mean.
SUBTLE   Or, gi't away: pox on't.
DAPPER
  I'll gi't mine aunt. I'll go and fetch the writings.   60
                                        [*Exit* DAPPER]
SUBTLE
  'Tis well, away.

                    [*Enter* FACE]

FACE   Where's Subtle?
SUBTLE   Here. What news?
FACE
  Drugger is at the door, go take his suit,
  And bid him fetch a parson, presently:
  Say, he shall marry the widow. Thou shalt spend
  A hundred pound by the service! [*Exit* SUBTLE] Now,
                                        queen Dol,   65
  Ha' you packed up all?
DOL   Yes.
FACE   And how do you like
  The lady Pliant?
DOL   A good dull innocent.

                    [*Enter* SUBTLE]

SUBTLE
  Here's your Hieronimo's cloak, and hat.
FACE   Give me 'em.
SUBTLE
  And the ruff too?
FACE   Yes, I'll come to you presently.
                                        [*Exit* FACE]

SUBTLE

    Now, he is gone about his project, Dol,   70
    I told you of, for the widow.

DOL   'Tis direct

    Against our articles.

SUBTLE   Well, we'll fit him, wench.
    Hast thou gulled her of her jewels, or her bracelets?

DOL

    No, but I will do't.

SUBTLE   Soon at night, my Dolly,
    When we are shipped, and all our goods aboard,   75
    Eastward for Ratcliff; we will turn our course
    To Brainford, westward, if thou saist the word:
    And take our leaves of this o'erweening rascal,
    This peremptory Face.

DOL   Content, I am weary of him.

SUBTLE

    Th' hast cause, when the slave will run a-wiving, Dol,   80
    Against the instrument, that was drawn between us.

DOL

    I'll pluck his bird as bare as I can.

SUBTLE   Yes, tell her,
    She must by any means, address some present
    To th' cunning man; make him amends, for wronging
    His art with her suspicion; send a ring;   85
    Or chain of pearl; she will be tortured else
    Extremely in her sleep, say: and ha' strange things
    Come to her. Wilt thou?

DOL   Yes.

SUBTLE   My fine flitter-mouse,
    My bird o'the night; we'll tickle it at the Pigeons,
    When we have all, and may unlock the trunks,   90
    And say, this's mine, and thine, and thine, and mine—

                 They kiss

            [*Enter* FACE]

FACE

    What now, a-billing?

SUBTLE   Yes, a little exalted
    In the good passage of our stock-affairs.

72 *we'll fit him* perhaps a glance at *The Spanish Tragedy*, **IV.i**, 70
77 *Brainford* Brentford, Middlesex
81 *instrument* agreement
88 *flitter-mouse* bat, term of endearment
89 *Pigeons* 'The Three Pigeons', an inn in Brentford market-place
93 *stock-affairs* joint venture

FACE

  Drugger has brought his parson, take him in, Subtle,
  And send Nab back again, to wash his face.   95
SUBTLE

  I will: and shave himself?
FACE   If you can get him. [*Exit* SUBTLE]
DOL

  You are hot upon it, Face, what e'er it is!
FACE

  A trick, that Dol shall spend ten pound a month by.

[*Enter* SUBTLE]

  Is he gone?
SUBTLE   The chaplain waits you i'the hall, sir.
FACE

  I'll go bestow him.   [*Exit* FACE]
DOL   He'll now marry her, instantly.   100
SUBTLE

  He cannot, yet, he is not ready. Dear Dol,
  Cozen her of all thou canst. To deceive him
  Is no deceit, but justice, that would break
  Such an inextricable tie as ours was.
DOL

  Let me alone to fit him.

[*Enter* FACE]

FACE   Come, my venturers,   105
  You ha' packed up all? Where be the trunks? Bring forth.
SUBTLE

  Here.
FACE   Let's see 'em. Where's the money?
SUBTLE   Here,
  In this.
FACE   Mammon's ten pound: eight score before.
  The Brethren's money, this. Drugger's, and Dapper's.
  What paper's that?
DOL   The jewel of the waiting maid's,   110
  That stole it from her lady, to know certain—
FACE

  If she should have precedence of her mistress?
DOL   Yes.
FACE

  What box is that?
SUBTLE   The fish wives' rings, I think:

And th' ale wives' single money. Is't not Dol?

DOL

Yes: and the whistle, that the sailor's wife   115
Brought to you, to know, and her husband were with Ward.

FACE

We'll wet it tomorrow: and our silver beakers,
And tavern cups. Where be the French petticoats,
And girdles, and hangers?

SUBTLE   Here, i' the trunk,
And the bolts of lawn.

FACE   Is Drugger's damask, there?   120
And the tobacco?

SUBTLE   Yes.

FACE   Give me the keys.

DOL

Why you the keys!

SUBTLE   No matter, Dol: because
We shall not open 'em, before he comes.

FACE

'Tis true, you shall not open them, indeed:
Nor have 'em forth. Do you see? Not forth, Dol.

DOL   No!   125

FACE

No, my smock-rampant. The right is, my master
Knows all, has pardoned me, and he will keep 'em.
Doctor, 'tis true (you look) for all your figures:
I sent for him, indeed. Wherefore, good partners,
Both he, and she, be satisfied: for, here   130
Determines the indenture tripartite,
Twixt Subtle, Dol, and Face. All I can do
Is to help you over the wall, o' the back-side;
Or lend you a sheet, to save your velvet gown, Dol.
Here will be officers, presently; bethink you,   135
Of some course suddenly to scape the dock:
For thither you'll come else.   *Some knock*
                          Hark you, thunder.

SUBTLE

You are a precious fiend!

OFFICER [*without*]   Open the door.

114 *single money* small change   120 *bolts* rolls of fabric
126 *right* truth of it   129 *I sent for him* not true, but a useful lie
131 *Determines* ends, is concluded

116 *Ward.* A famous Mediterranean pirate, whose base was at Tunis. He is
  mentioned in several plays of the period, and Daborne's *A Christian
  turned Turk*, 1612, is based, in part, on his exploits.

FACE

    Dol, I am sorry for thee i' faith. But hearst thou?

    It shall go hard, but I will place thee somewhere: 140

    Thou shalt ha' my letter to mistress Amo.

DOL   Hang you—

FACE

    Or madam Cæsarean.

DOL   Pox upon you, rogue,

    Would I had but time to beat thee.

FACE   Subtle,

    Let's know where you set up next; I'll send you

    A customer, now and then, for old acquaintance: 145

    What new course ha' you?

SUBTLE   Rogue, I'll hang myself:

    That I may walk a greater devil, than thou,

    And haunt thee i' the flock-bed, and the buttery.

                                [*Exeunt* SUBTLE, FACE, DOL]

Act V, Scene v

[*Enter*] LOVEWIT [, PARSON]

LOVEWIT

    What do you mean, my masters?

MAMMON [*without*]   Open your door,

    Cheaters, bawds, conjurers.

OFFICER [*without*]   Or we'll break it open.

LOVEWIT

    What warrant have you?

OFFICER   Warrant enough, sir, doubt not:

    If you'll not open it.

LOVEWIT   Is there an officer, there?

OFFICER

    Yes, two, or three for failing.

LOVEWIT   Have but patience,   5

    And I will open it straight.

[*Enter* FACE]

FACE   Sir, ha' you done?

    Is it a marriage? Perfect?

LOVEWIT   Yes, my brain.

141–2 *mistress Amo . . . madam Cæsarean* two brothel-keepers (Q
    reads 'Imperiall' for 'Cæsarean')
148 i.e. while you sleep and eat
  5 *for failing* as a precaution against failure

FACE

Off with your ruff, and cloak then, be yourself, sir.

SURLY [*without*]

Down with the door.

KASTRIL [*without*]   'Slight, ding it open.

LOVEWIT   Hold.

Hold gentlemen, what means this violence?   10

[*Enter* MAMMON, SURLY, KASTRIL, ANANIAS, TRIBULATION,
OFFICERS]

MAMMON

Where is this collier?

SURLY   And my Captain Face?

MAMMON

These day-owls.

SURLY   That are birding in men's purses.

MAMMON

Madam Suppository.

KASTRIL   Doxy, my suster.

ANANIAS   Locusts

Of the foul pit.

TRIBULATION   Profane as Bel, and the dragon.

ANANIAS

Worse than the grasshoppers, or the lice of Egypt.   15

LOVEWIT

Good gentlemen, hear me. Are you officers,

And cannot stay this violence?

OFFICER   Keep the peace.

LOVEWIT

Gentlemen, what is the matter? Whom do you seek?

MAMMON

The chemical cozener.

SURLY   And the Captain pander.

KASTRIL

The nun my suster.

MAMMON   Madam Rabbi.

ANANIAS   Scorpions,   20

And caterpillars.

LOVEWIT   Fewer at once, I pray you.

9 *ding* break   11 *collier* see I.i, 90 note
14 *Bel, and the dragon* from the book in the *Apocrypha*
17 *stay* control
20 *nun* facetious term for a prostitute

---

13 *Madam Suppository*. An apt word, since it not only refers to her study
of medicine but was a cant term for 'prostitute'.

OFFICER
   One after another, gentleman, I charge you,
   By virtue of my staff—
ANANIAS   They are the vessels
   Of pride, lust, and the cart.
LOVEWIT   Good zeal, lie still,
   A little while.
TRIBULATION   Peace, deacon Ananias.   25
LOVEWIT
   The house is mine here, and the doors are open:
   If there be any such persons, as you seek for,
   Use your authority, search on o' God's name.
   I am but newly come to town, and finding
   This tumult 'bout my door (to tell you true)   30
   It somewhat mazed me; till my man, here, (fearing
   My more displeasure) told me he had done
   Somewhat an insolent part, let out my house
   (Belike, presuming on my known aversion
   From any air o' the town, while there was sickness) 35
   To a Doctor, and a Captain: who, what they are,
   Or where they be, he knows not.
MAMMON   Are they gone?

                    They enter

LOVEWIT
   You may go in, and search, sir. Here, I find
   The empty walls, worse than I left 'em, smoked,
   A few cracked pots, and glasses, and a furnace,   40
   The ceiling filled with poesies of the candle:
   And madam, with a dildo, writ o' the walls.
   Only, one gentlewoman, I met here,
   That is within, that said she was a widow—
KASTRIL
   Ay, that's my suster. I'll go thump her. Where is she? 45
LOVEWIT
   And should ha' married a Spanish count, but he,
   When he came to't, neglected her so grossly,
   That I, a widower, am gone through with her.
SURLY
   How! Have I lost her then?
LOVEWIT   Were you the Don, sir?
   Good faith, now, she does blame y'extremely, and says 50

31 *mazed* amazed, puzzled
41 *poesies of the candle* marks made by candle smoke
42 *dildo* phallus

You swore, and told her, you had ta'en the pains,
To dye your beard, and umbre o'er your face,
Borrowed a suit, and ruff, all for her love;
And then did nothing. What an oversight,
And want of putting forward, sir, was this!   55
Well fare an old harquebuzier, yet,
Could prime his powder, and give fire, and hit,
All in a twinkling.

MAMMON   The whole nest are fled!
                    Mammon comes forth

LOVEWIT
What sort of birds were they?

MAMMON   A kind of choughs,
Or thievish daws, sir, that have picked my purse   60
Of eight score, and ten pounds, within these five weeks,
Beside my first materials; and my goods,
That lie i' the cellar: which I am glad they ha' left.
I may have home yet.

LOVEWIT   Think you so, sir?

MAMMON   Ay.

LOVEWIT
By order of law, sir, but not otherwise.   65

MAMMON
Not mine own stuff?

LOVEWIT   Sir, I can take no knowledge,
That they are yours, but by public means.
If you can bring certificate, that you were gulled of 'em,
Or any formal writ, out of a court,
That you did cozen yourself: I will not hold them.   70

MAMMON
I'll rather lose 'em.

LOVEWIT   That you shall not, sir,
By me, in troth. Upon these terms they are yours.
What should they ha' been, sir, turned into gold all?

MAMMON   No.
I cannot tell. It may be they should. What then?

LOVEWIT
What a great loss in hope have you sustained?   75

56 *harquebuzier* musketeer, armed with an 'harquebus', the fore-
   runner of the rifle
59 *choughs* birds of the crow family
67 *public means* course of law

---

61 *these five weeks*. This agrees, more or less, with V.i, 28–9, but the experiments of II.i, 5 have taken ten months. See Herford and Simpson
   for a discussion of the play's time-scheme.

MAMMON

Not I, the Commonwealth has.

FACE   Ay, he would ha' built
The city new; and made a ditch about it
Of silver, should have run with cream from Hogsden:
That, every Sunday in Moorfields, the younkers,
And tits, and tomboys should have fed on, *gratis*.   80

MAMMON

I will go mount a turnip cart, and preach
The end o' the world, within these two months. Surly,
What! In a dream?

SURLY   Must I needs cheat myself,
With that same foolish vice of honesty!
Come let us go, and harken out the rogues.   85
That Face I'll mark for mine, if e'er I meet him.

FACE

If I can hear of him, sir, I'll bring you word,
Unto your lodging: for in troth, they were strangers
To me, I thought 'em honest, as myself, sir.

                              [*Exeunt* MAMMON, SURLY]

TRIBULATION

'Tis well, the Saints shall not lose all yet. Go,   90
                    They come forth
And get some carts—

LOVEWIT   For what, my zealous friends?

ANANIAS

To bear away the portion of the righteous,
Out of this den of thieves.

LOVEWIT   What is that portion?

ANANIAS

The goods, sometimes the orphan's, that the Brethren,
Bought with their silver pence.

LOVEWIT   What, those i' the cellar,   95
The knight Sir Mammon claims?

ANANIAS   I do defy
The wicked Mammon, so do all the Brethren,
Thou profane man. I ask thee, with what conscience
Thou canst advance that idol, against us,
That have the seal? Were not the shillings numbered,   100
That made the pounds? Were not the pounds told out,
Upon the second day of the fourth week,

79 *younkers* children
80 *tits, and tomboys* young girls
85 *harken out* find out by enquiry
100 *That have the seal?* see, for example, *Revelation* ix,4

In the eighth month, upon the table dormant,
The year, of the last patience of the Saints,
Six hundred and ten.

LOVEWIT   Mine earnest vehement botcher,   105
And deacon also, I cannot dispute with you,
But, if you get you not away the sooner,
I shall confute you with a cudgel.

ANANIAS   Sir.

TRIBULATION
Be patient Ananias.

ANANIAS   I am strong,
And will stand up, well girt, against an host,   110
That threaten Gad in exile.

LOVEWIT   I shall send you
To Amsterdam, to your cellar.

ANANIAS   I will pray there,
Against thy house: may dogs defile thy walls,
And wasps, and hornets breed beneath thy roof,
This seat of falsehood, and this cave of cozenage.   115

                    [*Exeunt* ANANIAS, TRIBULATION]
          Drugger enters, and he beats him away

LOVEWIT
Another too?

DRUGGER   Not I sir, I am no Brother.

LOVEWIT
Away you Harry Nicholas, do you talk?   [*Exit* DRUGGER]

FACE
No, this was Abel Drugger. Good sir, go,
                    To the Parson
And satisfy him; tell him, all is done:
He stayed too long a-washing of his face.   120
The Doctor, he shall hear of him at Westchester;
And of the Captain, tell him at Yarmouth: or
Some good port town else, lying for a wind.   [*Exit Parson*]
If you get off the angry child, now, sir—

---

103 *table dormant* permanent side table, as distinct from the moveable
     'board'
111 *Gad in exile* HS suggest an allusion to *Genesis* xlix,19
121 *Westchester* modern Chester

---

117 *Harry Nicholas*. Henrick Niclaes (fl. 1502–1580), a native of Munster,
     was an Anabaptist and the leader of the sect called 'The Family of Love'
     (see Mosheim, *Ecclesiastical History*, IV.vii).   He came to England
     during the reign of Edward VI, and his pamphlets were translated into
     English by Christopher Vittel, a Southwark joiner. Queen Elizabeth
     issued a proclamation against the sect in 1580.

[*Enter* KASTRIL, DAME PLIANT]

KASTRIL

    Come on, you ewe, you have matched most sweetly, ha'

                            you not?   125

                To his sister

    Did not I say, I would never ha' you tupped

    But by a dubbed boy, to make you a lady tom?

    'Slight, you are a mammet! O, I could touse you, now.

    Death, mun' you marry with a pox?

LOVEWIT   You lie, boy;

    As sound as you: and I am aforehand with you.

KASTRIL   Anon?   130

LOVEWIT

    Come, will you quarrel? I will feeze you, sirrah.

    Why do you not buckle to your tools?

KASTRIL   God's light!

    This is a fine old boy, as e'er I saw!

LOVEWIT

    What, do you change your copy, now? Proceed,

    Here stands my dove: stoop at her, if you dare.   135

KASTRIL

    'Slight I must love him! I cannot choose, i' faith!

    And I should be hanged for't. Suster, I protest,

    I honour thee, for this match.

LOVEWIT   O, do you so, sir?

KASTRIL

    Yes, and thou canst take tobacco, and drink, old boy,

    I'll give her five hundred pound more, to her marriage,   140

    Than her own state.

LOVEWIT   Fill a pipe-full, Jeremy.

FACE

    Yes, but go in, and take it, sir.

LOVEWIT   We will.

    I will be ruled by thee in anything, Jeremy.

KASTRIL

    'Slight, thou art not hidebound! Thou art a jovy boy!

    Come let's in, I pray thee, and take our whiffs.   145

126 *tupped* mated, carrying on the 'farm' metaphor
128 *mammet* puppet; *touse* beat
131 *feeze you* frighten you off
132 *buckle to your tools* draw your weapon
134 *your copy* your style of behaviour
135 *stoop* swoop like a hawk (technical term in falconry)
144 *jovy* jovial

LOVEWIT

Whiff in with your sister, brother boy.
                    [*Exeunt* KASTRIL, DAME PLIANT]
                                        That master
That had received such happiness by a servant,
In such a widow, and with so much wealth,
Were very ungrateful, if he would not be
A little indulgent to that servant's wit,   150
And help his fortune, though with some small strain
Of his own candour. Therefore, gentlemen,
And kind spectators, if I have outstripped
An old man's gravity, or strict canon, think
What a young wife, and a good brain may do: 155
Stretch age's truth sometimes, and crack it too.
Speak for thyself, knave.

FACE   So I will, sir. Gentlemen,
My part a little fell in this last scene,
Yet 'twas decorum. And though I am clean
Got off, from Subtle, Surly, Mammon, Dol,   160
Hot Ananias, Dapper, Drugger, all
With whom I traded; yet I put myself
On you, that are my country: and this pelf,
Which I have got, if you do quit me, rests
To feast you often, and invite new guests.   165

THE END

152 *candour* fair reputation
162–3 *I put myself . . . country* a reference to the legal description of a
        jury
164 *quit* acquit

TEXTUAL NOTES

Dedication

2–3 *DESERVING . . . BLOOD* most æquall with vertue, and her Blood: The Grace, and Glóry of women Q

10–12 *Or, how . . . virtue?* Or how, yet, might a gratefull minde be furnish'd against the iniquitie of Fortune; except, when she fail'd it, it had power to impart it selfe? A way found out, to overcome euen those, whom Fortune hath enabled to returne most, since they, yet leaue themselues more. In this assurance am I planted; and stand with those affections at this Altar, as shall no more auoide the light and witnesse, then they doe the conscience of your vertue Q

14 *value of it, which* valew, that Q

15 *as the times are* in these times Q

17 *assiduity* daylinesse Q

18 *This, yet* But this Q

To the Reader

1 *To the Reader . . . than composed* Q; not in F

The Persons of the Play

1 *Play* Comœdie Q

14 **The Scene** *LONDON* F; not in Q

Prologue

10 *for* to Q

I.i

51 *you're* yo'were F (also I.ii, 128; I.iii, 51; IV.vi, 7) you were Q

69 *our state of grace* the high state of grace Q

114 *it* not in Q

149 *Death on me* Gods will Q

I.ii

45 *Dogs-meat* Dogges-mouth Q

56 *Xenophon* Testament Q

135 *Jove* Gad Q

I.iii

44 *metoposcopy* metaposcopie Q, F

67 *mercurial* Mercurian Q

147

I.iv

16 *possessed* possess'd on't Q

II.i

11 *the young* my yong Q
30 *thy* my Q, perh. correctly

II.ii

13 *Buy* Take Q
58 *They will . . . all others* not in Q
60 *pure* best Q

II.iii

18 *Now* No Q, F
25 SURLY SVB. Q
176 *metals* mettall Q
221–2 transposed in Q
249 *Eulen* Zephyrus Q
259 *her–wit–* / *Or so* her– / Wit? or so Q
260 SUBTLE *Eulen* not in Q SUBTLE not in F
272 SURLY SVB. Q, F
315 *Eulen* not in Q

II.iv
nil

II.v

10 *styptic* stipstick Q, F, (perh. intentionally to indicate Subtle's own error)

II.vi

25 FACE not in Q

III.i

2–4 *we of the . . . Sent forth* th'Elect must beare, with patience; / They are the exercises of the Spirit, / And sent Q

III.ii

36 *talc* Talek F
99 *glorious* holy Q
135 *you'll* you shall Q
142 *have a trick* F2; have trick Q, F

III.iii

22 *milk* feele Q
62 FACE F2; not in Q, F
79 *Let's* Lett's vs Q

III.iv

  4 (*he says.*) not in Q
  8 DRUGGER NAB. Q, E
  9 *Nab* not in Q
 75 *'Od's* God's Q
132 *go* go, sir Q

III.v
nil

IV.i

 18 *Eulen* Lungs Q
101 *solecism* solæcisme Q, F
107 *the light* light Q
112 *in* of Q
171 *laboratory* labaratory F

IV.ii
nil

IV.iii

 11 *'Slight* 'Sblood Q
 21 ff. Surly's Spanish has been corrected and modernized throughout

IV.iv

  3 FACE Q; not in F

IV.v

 25, 29 MAMMON MAN. F
 27 *Heber's* Helens Q, F
    With the Which the Q
 31 *fæces* fœces Q, F
 42 *stood still* gone back Q
 43 *gone back* stand still Q
 51 *This'll retard* This will hinder Q
 74 *voluptuous* voluptuouos F

IV.vi

 16 SURLY SVB. F

IV.vii

 32 *he's* he hath Q
104 SUBTLE SVR. F
126 *there* then Q

V.i

 29 NEIGHBOUR 1 ed. Q, F omit 1

V.ii
nil

V.iii
  44 *sulphur, sons of fire* Vipers, Sonnes of Belial Q
  45 *stench, it* wickednesse Q
  46 *Ay*, not in Q
  48 *Yes*, I (*i.e.*, Ay) Q

V.iv
  23 *you* her Q
  50 *and* if Q
  55 *twelve* fiue Q
  58 *your* Q; you F
  59 *pox* A pox Q
  60 DAPPER FAC. Q, F
  95 *Nab* him Q
 138 SUBTLE SYB. F
 142 *Cæsarean* Imperiall Q

V.v
  13 *suster* Q; sister F
  24 *pride, lust, and the cart* shame, and of dishonour Q
  32 *he* ed.; not in Q, F
  99 *idol* Nemrod Q
 116 s.d. at 118 F
 124 *get* can get Q
 145 *I* not in Q

Printed in Great Britain by
Fletcher & Son Ltd, Norwich